*Fresh Expressions of Church and the
Kingdom of God*

ANCIENT FAITH, FUTURE MISSION

Fresh Expressions of Church and the Kingdom of God

Edited by
Graham Cray,
Ian Mobsby
and Aaron Kennedy

CANTERBURY
PRESS
Norwich

© The Editors and Contributors 2012

First published in 2012 by the Canterbury Press Norwich
Editorial office
3rd Floor, Invicta House,
108–114 Golden Lane,
London EC1Y OTG.

Canterbury Press is an imprint of Hymns Ancient & Modern Ltd
(a registered charity)
13A Hellesdon Park Road, Norwich,
Norfolk, NR6 5DR, UK

www.canterburypress.co.uk

British Library Cataloguing in Publication data

A catalogue record for this book is available
from the British Library

978 1 84825 091 8

Typeset by Regent Typesetting, London
Printed and bound in Great Britain by
CPI Group (UK) Ltd, Reading

Contents

List of Contributors

Rowan Williams was enthroned as Archbishop of Canterbury in February 2003. His previous positions include Archbishop of Wales, Lady Margaret Professor of Divinity, Oxford, and Dean of Clare College, Cambridge. He has taught theology for more than fifteen years in five continents, worked as a parish priest, and published widely. His previous publications include *Dostoyevsky: Language, Faith and Fiction* (2008) and *Silence and Honey Cakes: The Wisdom of the Desert* (2003).

Graham Cray is the Archbishops' Missioner and Leader of the UK Fresh Expressions Team. He was previously Bishop of Maidstone in the Diocese of Canterbury, and Principal of Ridley Hall, Cambridge. He chaired the working party that wrote the *Mission-shaped Church* report, which coined the term 'Fresh Expressions of Church', and he is the chair of the panel that interviews potential Ordained Pioneer Ministers for the Church of England.

Richard Sudworth is a Pioneer curate of the Church of England in a Muslim-majority part of Birmingham. He worked for ten years for the Church Mission Society in North Africa and Birmingham before ordination, and is the author of *Distinctly Welcoming: Christian Presence in a Multifaith Society* (Scripture Union, 2007). Richard is a PhD candidate at Heythrop College, University of London.

Paul Kennedy balances inherited Church as Rector of East Winchester with being part of the emerging community Refresh. Paul is also a Benedictine oblate at Alton Abbey, and looks for ways of bringing ancient teachings on community and hospitality to the estates, town houses and countryside of eastern Winchester. Married to Paula, a science teacher, with three teenage sons, most of his time reflecting is spent on a surfboard off the Cornish coast; or, when Cornwall is too far away, cycling the Hampshire Downs. Paul has previously enjoyed the City of London and atheism with varying degrees of success, and loves fine coffee – so would be happy to meet for an espresso.

The Revd Nadia Bolz-Weber is the founding pastor of House for All Sinners and Saints, a Lutheran church in Denver, Colorado. She is the author of *Salvation on the Small Screen? 24 Hours of Christian Television* (2008, Seabury), and blogs at www.sarcasticlutheran.com and Jim Wallis's www.Godspolitics.com. Her writings can be found in *The Christian Century, The Lutheran Magazine* and Patheos.com. She may be a leading voice in the emerging church, but nobody really believes she's an ordained pastor in the Evangelical Lutheran Church in America. Maybe it's the sleeve tattoos or the fact that she swears like a truck driver. Either way ... she's fine with it. Nadia lives in Denver with her family of four.

Phyllis Tickle, the founding editor of the Religion Department of *Publishers Weekly*, is an authority on Emergence Christianity. A popular lecturer in the history and sociology of the twenty-first-century Church, she is the author of some two dozen books, including the best-selling *The Great Emergence* and *The Divine Hours* series of manuals for observing the Daily Offices. With her physician husband, she makes her home on a small farm in Lucy, Tennessee.

Paul Paynter is married to Kerry and they have two sons, Noah and Ezra. Paul has been serving at Christian Family Centre (NI) in County Antrim, Northern Ireland, since 1998. You can find out more at www.cfc-armoy.org or email Paul at paul@cfc-armoy.org.

Diana Greenfield is a Pioneer priest and a Church Army Officer. She is currently serving her curacy in Glastonbury and is the Ordained Pioneer Minister for Avalon (the Church of England benefices of Street and Glastonbury). From 2000 to 2008 she pioneered nightclub chaplaincy ministries in Bournemouth and Maidstone, and contributed to *Young People and Mission* (Church House Publishing, 2007). She holds MAs in Theology and Mission from York St John and in Theology and Ministry from King's College, London. She is passionate to find ways of making the Kingdom of God accessible to those who are perceived as being far away. She is married to Sedge and they have four cats and a dog.

The Revd Lincoln Harvey is Tutor in Theology at St Mellitus College, London. He is also Associate Priest at St Andrew's Fulham Fields, having served his curacy at St John-at-Hackney in East London.

Andy Freeman lives in Reading and works with 24-7 Prayer, developing new monastic rhythms of life and prayer for the movement, including authoring *Punk Monk*. Andy is also training as a Pioneer Ordinand in the Church of England and works with CMS in Oxford, supporting Pioneers across the South of England. He is part of the Fresh Expressions national team for the UK. Andy is a divorced father of five kids, three of whom are now at university. Andy loves Indie and Punk music, enjoys reading and the arts, and is most at home with a pint of ale, watching cricket.

The Revd Michael Angell is the Assistant Rector at St John's Church, Lafayette Square, in Washington, DC. He is responsible for ministry with young adults and the Latino congregation. Before St John's, he served for two years as the Campus Missioner to the University of California at San Diego, replanting campus ministry there for the Episcopal Church. In his second year at UCSD, Mike was selected by his fellow campus ministers to receive the Sam Portaro award, the national honour for campus ministry in the Episcopal Church.

Damian Feeney is Vice-Principal and Charles Marriott Director of Pastoral Studies at St Stephen's House, Oxford, and an associate member of the University of Oxford Faculty of Theology. Prior to 2009 he was a parish priest and missioner in the Diocese of Blackburn, and was a member of the working party that produced the original *Mission-shaped Church* report. He is a member of the Leading Your Church into Growth team and the College of Evangelists, having initiated eucharistic church plants in Harrogate and Preston; he is also a member of the Society of the Holy Cross. He is married to Fiona, a church primary school head teacher, and they have three grown-up children.

Toby Wright is the Team Rector of Witney. He also serves as a diocesan Missioner in the Diocese of Oxford. Before this post, Toby was parish priest of Saint John Chrysostom with Saint Andrew in Peckham, South London, and Area Dean of Camberwell. He is a former chair of Fresh Expressions Roundtable 5. Previously, he read theology at New College, Oxford, having worked as a researcher for the Westminster Ethical Policy Forum and as a pastoral assistant at a school on a Peabody Estate in London. After undertaking priestly formation at the College of the Resurrection, Mirfield, Toby served his curacy in Petersfield in Hampshire. Toby is married to Sally, who is also ordained; they have a son, Caspar, and a daughter, Felicity.

Clare Catford is a journalist and has spent twenty years presenting and reporting for the UK's major television and radio networks. She currently works as a host of the *Guardian*'s news podcasts and is a regular contributor to Radio 2's *Pause for Thought* and Radio 4's *Beyond Belief*. She has also hosted *Reporting Religion* on the BBC's World Service and won a national award for best BBC faith documentary in 2008. She has an MA in Pastoral Theology, specializing in Mental Health and Spirituality, and a Post-graduate Diploma in Theology from King's College, London, majoring in Christian Ethics, Islam and Anthropology. Her first book, *Addicted to Love: From Rehab to Heaven?*, was published by Darton, Longman & Todd in 2008. She is a regular speaker at the Greenbelt Arts Festival. www.clarecatford.co.uk.

The Revd Samuel Wells is Vicar of St Martin-in-the-Fields, London. Much of his ministry has focused on contexts and issues of social disadvantage. He is the author of seventeen books, including works on Christian ethics such as *Improvisation* (Brazos, 2004) and *God's Companions* (Blackwell, 2006), and more popular works such as *Power and Passion* (Zondervan, 2007), *Living Without Enemies* (with Marcia A. Owen, Inter-Varsity Press, 2011), *What Anglicans Believe* (Canterbury, 2011), and *Be Not Afraid* (Brazos, 2011).

Introduction

'The time is fulfilled, and the kingdom of God has come near; repent, and believe in the good news.' (Mark 1.15)

Whether we like it or not there is a tension between the words 'church' and the 'Kingdom of God'. At a very simplistic level the word church concerns the call of all Christians to be gathered as a spiritual community to worship and serve God together; where the Kingdom of God concerns the world where God is at work bringing justice, reconciliation and restoration between God and all life, with Christians responding to the call to join in with that work.

A good example of this tension is how Jesus and Paul use these terms. In the Gospel texts[1] Jesus mentions the 'Kingdom of God' fifty-three times in all the passages, but only mentions the word 'church' four times in the Gospel of Matthew. However, at the same time, Paul, in the New Testament letters largely attributed to him, uses the words associated with 'church' sixty-one times, and Kingdom of God seventeen times. Some writers have inferred from such observations that the kingdom seems to matter more to Jesus than the Church, and that for Paul, the Church seems to be more important than the Kingdom of God.

This has been reflected until very recently in the division between Church and para-church, non-profit and mission organizations. Churches were seen to address the ministry, worship and pastoral care needs of people from a particular church community and in the local parish context. At the same time para-church, non-profit and mission organizations were concerned with mission, evangelism and justice-orientated work in the world outside the Church and the specific geography of parish. This overly simplistic binary has not been unhelpful and is the cause of a great many divisions in the modern Church.

For those whose faith practice is grounded in a high view of Church, there is a deep distrust of those whose centre of gravity is in mission, with the concern that such people are in danger of 'dumbing down' on Church and its traditions. For those who have a higher regard for the Kingdom of God, there is a great concern that Church can institutionalize and withdraw Christians from real connection and involvement in the world outside the 'bubble' of Church.

This division has extended even to those who reflect on theology. Those who have a high regard for the Church tend to feel that ecclesiology is more important than missiology, which might be looked down upon as being less academic. At the same time, the more kingdom focused emphasize that missiology is far more important than ecclesiology, which is looked down upon as being out of touch with the real world.

This binary has characterized the debate around fresh expressions in general, and the *Mission-shaped Church* report in particular. Those espousing a high view of Church have argued that its title should have been *Church-shaped Mission* report, while those who see the kingdom and the world as more important than the Church have defended the original title.

The truth is that both the Church and the Kingdom of God are important and related in God's purposes. Bishop Steven Croft put this well when, in the first volume of the *Ancient Faith Future Mission* series, he described fresh expressions of church as 'building ecclesial communities out of contextual mission'. In so doing, Bishop Croft opens up the call for Christians to be involved in loving service in the world, listening and responding to God's call and social need, with the hope that expressions of Church will grow out of such action. This is after all part of our apostolic calling – the gathering of the people of God as Church who are then sent into the world. Where there is an over emphasis on Church there is the accompanying danger that the Church will fail to grow into its apostolic calling – if it only gathers for worship but is never sent into the world. This prevents Christians from exploring the full range of implications of Christian discipleship. By the same token, if the people of God are just involved in mission and evangelism without gathering as Church and participating in collective worship, we will also be impoverished, lacking the rootedness and sacramentality worship brings to our common life.

This book seeks to take a non-dual and integrated approach to holding both Church and the Kingdom of God in tension. It tells the story of how fresh expressions of Church have sought to address some of the really complex and difficult issues of life in the real world, while also coming together in worship and knowing the Church community as a deep spiritual home.

We also remember that the 'Five Marks of Mission' are deeply held by Anglicans, Methodists and Churches Together UK. These marks also cross the boundary between Church and kingdom. They have been summarized as:

To proclaim the Good News of the Kingdom.
To teach, baptize and nurture new believers.
To respond to human need by loving service.
To seek to transform unjust structures of society.
To strive to safeguard the integrity of creation and sustain and renew the life of the earth.

(Bonds of Affection-1984 ACC-6 p49, Mission in a Broken World-1990 ACC-8 p101)

We remember the important message from Jesus in the Gospel of Luke, which teaches that the kingdom is mystically present inside and around each of us. We are the Church, and the kingdom is present in each of us. This is an incredible spiritual reality and gift from God that we often neglect.

Once Jesus was asked by the Pharisees when the kingdom of God was coming, and he answered, 'The kingdom of God is not coming with things that can be observed; nor will they say, "Look, here it is!" or "There it is!" For, in fact, the kingdom of God is among you.' (Luke 17.20–21)

Finally, we would like to thank those who have helped make this – the third book in the *Ancient Faith Future Mission* series – possible. Our thanks go to: Aaron Kennedy our co-editor and copy editor; Christine Smith and her team at Canterbury Press for their ongoing support and interest in this series, and to the many contributing authors who have made this book possible.

Bishop Graham Cray
Ian Mobsby
Aaron Kennedy

Note

1 According to the New Revised Standard Version.

Fresh Expressions, the Cross and the Kingdom

ARCHBISHOP ROWAN WILLIAMS

One of the sharpest criticisms of the new look in mission represented by fresh expressions – that new look with which, I stress at the outset, I am in entire sympathy – is that it accepts without challenge a private and apolitical perspective that simply colludes with the general culture of consumer choice and the search for what makes me feel better rather than what is true. It is really a two-pronged challenge: on the one hand, where is the cross, the emptying and reshaping of the self by radical grace? On the other, where is the Kingdom, the hope for a transformed society and world, not just an improved network of religiosity? In these pages, I want to attempt a response – not a case-by-case justification of all that goes on under the FX banner, but a reflection on how the practice of FX can and must do justice to these questions and how it can help the historic mainstream of the Church recognize its problems more clearly and courageously as well.

Let me begin with one or two observations on the New Testament Church. It's clear that the 'assembly' that constitutes itself around the Risen Jesus when the good news is proclaimed is distinguished not only by what it 'confesses', what it states as true and authoritative, but by the character of its relations – 'life in the Spirit', marked by mutual patience, generosity and interdependence (e.g. Gal. 5.22 ff.). But because life in the Spirit is simply life in Christ – since the characteristic prayer of the person living in the Spirit is the 'Abba, Father' of Jesus in his agony in Gethsemane (Rom. 8.15, Gal. 4.6) – it is clear at once that the patience, generosity and mutuality of the Spirit-filled community rests on a continuing erosion of what have become our instinctive habits of reacting to others (what Paul calls 'the flesh'). The character of Christian relations takes for granted both a gift and a discipline: the gift of being caught up into the life of Jesus as he advances towards cross and glory, and the discipline of scrutinizing yourself for the marks of surviving selfishness.

This immediately poses a challenge to any and every Christian community. Have we succeeded in creating a Christian group in which each individual member is living by some degree of mutual patience and generosity and yet which *as a whole* gives off an air of exclusion and self-absorption? We do not take up Christ's cross just for the sake of living more fruitfully with our believing neighbours, simply because Christ's cross is something that he takes up for the sake of the entire world. So individual humility and corporate arrogance or self-satisfaction is not a defensible mixture for a biblical Church. If my membership of the Christian community is not just about what makes me as an individual feel better, the Christian community itself cannot be aimed only at a collective 'feeling better'.

This is where fresh expressions of Church life have both huge positive potential and huge capacity for misunderstanding. The positive potential is in the fact that fresh expressions begin from a creative dissatisfaction with aspects of inherited patterns of Church life, sensing that they may have become self-serving, to the extent that they will reinforce what their members already think and feel. The new mission agenda seeks to take seriously the *strangeness* of the world at large. It accepts that in order to speak the Word of God effectively in an unfamiliar context, you will have to let the Word of God itself become 'strange' to you and discover it all over again in someone else's language and culture. It is therefore well-placed to resist the idea that the Church as a community can be content with a sort of internal equilibrium or harmony while doing nothing to carry the cross collectively, to empty itself sacrificially for the sake of the world that has not yet properly heard the good news.

On the other hand, the risk of misunderstanding comes from the possible alliance between a fresh expressions agenda and a sort of religious consumerism. 'Inherited' Church does not satisfy an individual's aspirations for fulfilment, so something new has to be tried. There can be a deeply unhelpful collusion between a generally individualistic culture and a Church that is losing confidence in its own distinctive calling or gift, leading to a desperate scramble to find 'acceptable' words or behaviours that will respond to a market demand. In other words, it is not only within the traditional forms of Church life that people can be trapped in a comfort zone, imagining that this is 'spiritual' existence.

So critics of the FX approach have a point when they observe the risk of eroding the element of sacrifice, of going beyond what 'feels' satisfying or fulfilling by paying the wrong kind of attention to the needs of a secular public. At worst, this ends up in the reduction of worship to entertainment, doctrine to comforting uplift and witness to marketing. And this spells the end of any real link with what the Church of the New Testament claims to be – which is the sacramental foreshadowing of humanity restored to the mutuality of love and service for which God intends it, life in the Spirit.

Life in the Spirit is not a 'spiritual life' in which certain specific spiritual needs are catered for, but life in the communion and solidarity that is the maximal expression of the image of God. God is revealed as Father, Son and Spirit, a life of irreducible difference and unqualified interdependence. For created persons, the calling is to let ourselves be drawn more and more deeply into dependence on God as Source and Father by deepening our relation with the incarnate Son, Jesus, a relation that is made effective by the sharing of Jesus' Spirit. In that renewed communion in and within the Trinity, our individuality is radically transformed so that we are made able to live in reciprocal love and gift. *The Church exists to manifest the new humanity, the restored image.* Once we forget this, we slip into just that fragmented picture of human existence that the gospel promises to deliver us from, with 'religion' or 'spirituality' as an activity among others that relates to an interest

3

or need among others. The point is memorably expressed by the great Anglican poet and novelist Charles Williams when, writing about the Kingdom of God as it appears in the gospels, he says that it is 'not a state of being without which one can get along very well. To lose it is to lose everything else' (p. 63).

So the challenge for any church community, 'inherited' or experimental, is going to be the same: how do we inhabit and understand its life so that we keep before us the call to show a comprehensive newness of human possibility? There are not going to be any crystal-clear methods to avoid error here, but I want to suggest three questions about church life that need careful attention as at least a basis for honest and faithful discipleship.

1 How does the community enable its members to grow in prayer so as to enter more fully into the central mystery of Christ's relationship with his Father? Teaching about prayer cannot just stop with exhortations to be confident about asking God for things. That in itself is, of course, perfectly biblical in one way, but it can – as in the more toe-curling varieties of prosperity gospel culture – become just another way of consumerizing faith. Nor can it stop with encouraging emotional intensity in devotion. There has to be some real help in stilling and opening the mind and heart to receive not just a set of feelings or a set of answers to prayer but an abiding *relation* to the Father in Jesus Christ. The community has to take it for granted that everyone is capable of growing; and the worst thing we can do is to go on treating people as less than spiritual adults.

2 Can the community point to something in its collective life that makes a contribution to the wider society which would not be made if there were no Christian presence around? In other words, can it point to a distinctive practice that shows in some area of public life that there are alternative ways of managing human relations or problems to the ones that prevail most widely in our culture? This may be something relatively modest – not every worshipping community will generate a Mother Teresa – even if it is only the free

provision of space for social needs or a programme of volunteering or the organizing of leisure activities for children
in a safe environment. The point is simply to show that
there is *something* specific that is happening as a result of
Christian commitment locally that can be pinned clearly to
a set of distinctive convictions about how human relations
should flourish.

3 How far does the community encourage and enable its
members to teach and to learn from one another? Is there
an atmosphere in which people can share what is genuinely
on their minds, without any sense that there is a blueprint
of acceptable behaviour or a standard level of 'spiritual'
attainment or stability against which they will be judged?
Mutuality, mutual service, has a lot to do with how believers work to build each other up, instead of concentrating
obsessively on 'how I'm doing' or being too embarrassed to
talk seriously about discipleship at all.

In all these ways, Christian communities challenge the corporate
imagination of their social context, seeking to nourish critical,
self-aware persons who are not afraid to be silent and receptive
before the mystery of God and not afraid to be engaged with
each other in exploring the new humanity they have discovered. They have moved beyond being consumers, being passive;
they are taking responsibility for becoming mature, with the
help and nurture of their community. So, looking back to the
risks identified earlier in both inherited and emerging styles of
Christian life, we can say that they are resisting entertainment,
marketing and uplift, the great temptations of an evangelisti-
cally minded Church in an unsympathetic environment.

At the heart of this is the belief that the good news cannot
be good news just for me as an individual. Evangelism must be
more than the invitation to find Christian faith an attractive
option for myself; that would be to shrink the universal impact
of the gospel. As soon as I hear the promise of grace for myself,
I hear the summons *to make my renewed life good news for the
neighbour and the stranger*. And this is of course just where
some of the distinctive emphases of FX come into their own

in a positive way. Good news has to be audible. It must be recognizable at least as *news*, and for that to happen there has to be real attention to how sense is being made in the context in which you are trying to communicate. This is very definitely not the same thing as simply looking for a more accessible way to express challenges or mysteries with the danger that the element of challenge and mystery melts away. It is a slow and patient exercise in discovering what can and can't be heard.

And it is very much in the mainstream tradition of Christian mission. Recently I was taking part in the celebrations of the 300th anniversary of the Indian SPCK, and was reminded of the way in which, in India as elsewhere, the actual translation of the Scriptures into local languages frequently had the effect of reviving the languages themselves, especially when they were the languages of oppressed or marginal groups. Suddenly, with the Bible available in their own language, such people found they had new things to say. It was not just that the Bible had been translated into their language; their language had been 'translated' into a new register, and so their lives changed. This kind of exchange or interaction is always a mark of mission doing its work; and a missionary 'translation' that does no more than look for vague equivalents of ideas and images, without actually galvanizing the new context, is failing. New humanity means newness in language; and if all that missional strategy achieves is ways of saying the same thing in less confident and challenging idioms, something is missing.

One of the most remarkable recent experiments in creating the reality of 'church' virtually from nothing was the project at Penrhys in the Rhondda Valley, led by John and Norah Morgans. In 1986, the Moderator of the URC in Wales and his wife chose to move to this destitute and profoundly troubled estate with the goal of nurturing the emergence of a genuinely local Christian community worship and service. The following eighteen years saw an extraordinary flowering of the life of the Spirit in Penrhys – not in the form of huge congregations or a classical revival, but in the shape of a steady transformation of expectations and horizons. Collaboration on the setting up of a health clinic, the use of the small worship space within the two converted houses that formed the church centre for concerts, popular and classical, by world-class performers, the growth of an international network of volunteers and supporters, the regular retreats with the Cistercian monks of Caldey Island for young people on the estate, even the simple fact of some teenagers deciding it was worth sitting their A-Levels – all this and a good deal more is described in John Morgans' diaries, published privately by him in 2008 as *Journey of a Lifetime*.[1] As a chronicle of how the Church 'translates' the expectations of the community in which it stands, how it defines and enables alternative life-choices for people trapped in any number of self-destructive patterns, it could not be bettered.

But it is not a chronicle of steady success. John Morgans is completely honest about the draining cost of keeping motivation alive in circumstances like these, and about the sense of 'two steps forward, one step back' (sometimes two steps back) that accompanied the development of ministry in Penrhys. 'Grasping the divine resources available for transforming personhood, relationships and community', he writes, 'demands constant patience. It is the work of maturing. It cannot be slick and it is always costly' (p. 442). But what is lastingly achieved is a different sense of possibility, the possibility of some kind of human wholeness – shown perhaps only fleetingly but setting a new horizon for what people can hope for. The basic characteristics of the life of Llanfair Penrhys, the church centre on the estate, had to do with communal ministry, service and depth of spiritual discipline (p. 443). The stress on communal ministry came from the recognition that ordained ministers in contexts like Penrhys – but in many other quite different contexts too – faced isolation and burnout; there had to be a mutually supportive core group at work. Service was an obvious imperative in a community desperately in need of a 'catalyst for change' (p. 458) but *not* in need of paternalistic solutions imposed from outside. And one of the most moving aspects of the diaries is the tracing of a greater and greater deepening of prayer, with help from, among others, the contemplative monks of Caldey – Roman Catholics who had no problems in wholeheartedly supporting a Welsh Nonconformist initiative.

Set alongside the three questions which I earlier suggested should be near the heart of the life of a mature and biblical community, Penrhys demonstrates dramatically what it means to live under such scrutiny. The centrality of the life of worship and the expectation that people would grow and *want* to grow spiritually are manifest throughout Morgans' narrative. The perceptible change in the environment, the change in what can be imagined and spoken of, is clear in countless stories of particular people finding unexpected extra dimensions to their lives. The neediness, the sense of urgency around deprivation and hopelessness, broke down inhibitions about sharing and supporting within the family of believers and would-be believers. Reading John Morgans – and seeing the work in Penrhys as I was privileged to do in the nineties – you could say (to borrow a phrase I have used elsewhere) 'I have seen the Church and it works.' Would you characterize Penrhys as 'inherited' or 'emergent'? I don't think the question could be answered; quite simply, it was a *church*: a community in which by the bearing of the cross of self-forgetfulness and mutuality, the new humanity was allowed by God's grace to be visible.

Some may hear at this point echoes of the scepticism expressed with memorable sharpness by Shane Claiborne, one of the pioneers of the 'new-monasticism' in the US. In his book in collaboration with John M. Perkins, *Follow Me to Freedom*, he articulates what might have been John Morgans' guiding insight on Penrhys: 'The inner city doesn't need more "churches"; it needs a Church, a Body, a people serving and working together as one family' (p. 202). He offers a defence of *local* identity for the Church as robust as anything that has come from British critics of fresh expressions in the name of the parochial ideal – and he also underscores the need for a clear ecclesiology behind this, an ecclesiology that connects with the sense of a whole global, even cosmic project that is God's work. 'I once heard someone say', he writes (p. 219), 'that all you need to start an "emerging church" is a Bible, a candle and a copy of the *Matrix* movie (and some would say the first two are optional). It seems that "emerging church" has become little more than a box where you can put anyone who is under 40 and has fresh ideas – and not have to listen to them.' In contrast, he insists on the need for a church to have a 'DNA', a theologically recognizable set of criteria for integrity and a web of relations with the cosmic project of God in Christ. And in a sense that is what this chapter is really all about: the DNA of Church that makes it more than entertainment, uplift and marketing, the genetic language of the cross in all that Christians do, and the shape of the new humanity that is created by the events of Easter.

'Ecclesiology' is a forbidding word, and some of the discussions that have gone on under this rubric have been forbidding enough in all conscience. But essentially what 'ecclesiology' means is the search to ground what we say about Church in what we say about God, the active God of Scripture, so that our understanding and expectations around church life and priorities are not left stranded in a welter of bright ideas about a human institution and how to promote it. Here, perhaps, is the most substantial and interesting challenge for the FX world. How do we keep the focus on the action of God, rather than on the choices and preferences of human agents? Because it is as we learn how to do this more consistently that we become better able to serve the Kingdom in the ways we've been discussing through the transformation of our social environment. God's world is not just an improved version of ours, but a radical alternative, and this will only stay alive as a vision if we are clear about the priority of his action towards us.

It is an area where the significance of the *sacraments* becomes clear, since they are celebrations and effective enactments of the acts of God. It has been said already by a fair number of commentators, but it bears saying again – FX is not an anti-sacramental style of life, even if it is sensitive and patient about how people are drawn in to the sacramental actions of the Church (again John Morgans has a lot to say about this). It may be surprising for some, but the truth is that when we have our sacramental teaching and practice clear, we are likely to have our transformational social vision clear as well. The sacraments show us, bring us into touch with, the God who acts before any initiative on our part; so they show us a God who is free from our preoccupations and agendas. Communion with this God of freedom sets us free to be critics and remakers of our world in his name.

To go back to an earlier point: one of the strengths of the FX vision is precisely to affirm the freedom of God – freedom from our comfort zones and our religiosity. At best, FX is grounded in learning new things about God from listening to what he is already doing, ahead of us, in the world he loves. It is, then, completely consistent with this emphasis to look for ways of keeping clear the sense of the God who is *ahead* of us. Having the sacramental question plainly in view is one such discipline; and rightly understood this helps us ask just those questions spelled out earlier in this chapter. Sacramental life is about that deep identification with Jesus crucified and risen that is always at work in us, however we are feeling and however we think we are doing. It affirms that there is a new world both promised and realized in our midst as we worship. And it reminds us that the solidarity between us is not a matter of human preference and convenience but the result of God's unpredictable call – so that every other person in our fellowship is there with a distinctive relation with God that is given to be shared with all. When we miss out on the liberty of God and make the unity of the Church a matter of our planning and control, of human agreement and compatibility, or of institutional neatness, we fail to set before our world the essential promise of humanity and creation renewed. We are wasting our time in a leisure activity designed to cultivate our religious feelings and our tribal loyalties.

FX can fall into these traps as surely as other forms of church life; being involved with a fresh expression or emerging church does not stop you being an averagely sinful or stupid human being. What matters is the biblical truth about new relations, the reality of *communion*, radical sharing between God and God's creation, and so between human persons and so between persons and the whole material order in which they are set. I have been arguing that FX is well-placed to keep the emphasis on the absolute priority of God's action, not ours, at the forefront of its thinking and practice, but also that it needs to sustain a self-questioning habit, along the lines sketched, and a sense of how the sacramental life of the community works to hold us faithful to the priority of an act that is not ours.

John Morgans, writing about the way in which the Church's liturgical year came alive in Penrhys, says that the effect of celebrating this liturgical round was that 'We knew where we were in time and space ... not alone, but together with God's People we are engaged in a life-long pilgrimage with an annual programme' (2008, p. 450). The point is of wider application than just the liturgical year. The Church of God does indeed seek to *locate* people in time and space, to make them inhabitants of a renewed reality. For this to happen, wherever and however the Church exists it must be asking itself how the new reality is made visible in particular lives and in the life of the whole community. Seeking to translate the good news afresh, it seeks at the same time to 'translate' the world around, to *re-locate* it in the context of God's new creation. The New Testament makes it plain that this only happens when we enter the stripping and re-creating process that is the living-out of baptism, the entry into cross and resurrection in our own particular lives. And beyond that is the constant costly patience of which John Morgans writes so movingly. After all, if our focus remains on the priority of God's action, our patience will always be sustained by hope for what we cannot see but know we can trust: the divine liberty that has set us free for service and celebration.

References

Shane Claiborne and John M. Perkins, 2009, *Follow Me to Freedom: Leading and Following as an Ordinary Radical*, Ventura, CA: Regal Books

John and Norah Morgans, 2008, *Journey of a Lifetime: From the Diaries of John Morgans*, privately published (ISBN 978-0-9560689-0-3)

Charles Williams, 1938, *He Came Down From Heaven*, London: Heinemann

Note

1 *Journey of a Lifetime: From the Diaries of John Morgans*, 2008, privately published by John and Norah Morgans, ISBN 978-0-9560689-0-3. It would be a great gift to the churches to have extracts at least of this wonderful document available through commercial publishing.

2

Communities of the Kingdom

BISHOP GRAHAM CRAY

> Church planting should not be church centred. It should not be another device to perpetuate an institution for that institution's sake. It is to be an expression of the mission of God. (*Mission-shaped Church*, 2004, p. 85)

The *Mission-shaped Church* report[1] has been subject to two mutually contradictory critiques. To John Hull it was deficient because it promoted a 'church-shaped mission' and made the Church the primary object of its own activity. To Andrew Davison, the report's emphasis on the Kingdom of God, as contrasted to the Church, was deflecting the Church from its calling as a vital part of the message it proclaims. As it happens, neither writer objects in principle to the local projects and mission initiatives in themselves. It is the theological justification and the terminology that is the focus of their criticisms. Most critiques are as much about the concerns their authors wish to safeguard as they are about the counter-points being made. Hull fears a Church concerned only with its own narrow agenda. Davison fears a diminished understanding of the role of the Church in God's salvation. I fully share both concerns.

The purpose of this chapter is not to refute critiques,[2] but to explore the relationship between the Church of God and the Kingdom of God, as that impacts upon the planting of fresh expressions of Church.

Church and kingdom interconnected

Contrasting statements about Church and kingdom can under-state their essential interconnection. There is a symbiotic relationship between the two. The Church is the body of Christ. The Kingdom is the Kingdom of Christ. Both are empty apart from the presence of Christ and the ministry of the Spirit of Christ. The Kingdom of God is 'creation healed' (Kung, 2006, p. 231). The Church is the community of redeemed human beings – created as stewards and priests of creation, fallen, but now restored to their stewardship in Christ. The kingdom is the rule of Christ over the whole creation. The Church is the community that has submitted to that rule and seeks to live under it, in the midst of a world that locates ultimate authority elsewhere. Both need to be understood from an eschatological perspective. Both are 'now and not yet'. The Church on earth is an imperfect community of people, still in the process of becoming like Christ. The kingdom is the presence of the new age, which has not yet displaced the old age. Both anticipate and look towards the new creation: 'the mutual indwelling of the triune God and his glorified people in a new heaven and earth' (Volf, 1998, p. 266).

Church and kingdom distinguished

Theologically it is still necessary to make the distinction between the Kingdom of God, as 'a divine activity', and the Church, as 'a human community' (*Mission-shaped Church*, p. 86). This is a fundamental New Testament distinction.

> The Kingdom is primarily the dynamic reign or kingly rule of God, and derivatively, the sphere in which the rule is experi-enced. In biblical idiom, the Kingdom is not identified with its subjects. They are the people of God's rule who enter it, live under it, and are governed by it. The church is the com-munity of the Kingdom but never the Kingdom itself. (Ladd, 1974, p. 262)

Christians hope for more than the Church. They hope for new heavens and a new earth, and for 'the kingdom of this world to become the kingdom of our Lord' (Rev. 11.15). They hope for the final destruction of evil and for the reconciliation of 'all things' in Christ. The people of God are not to be confused with 'the totality of the reign of God'. Even after the consummation the distinction needs to be sustained. 'Despite their relationship with one another the glorified people of God and the glorified world of God are to be distinguished' (Volf, 1998, p. 267). In this age, 'As a human entity, the Church is marked by all the ambiguity and frailty of the human condition and is constantly in need of repentance, reform and renewal' (House of Bishops, 1997, 2.12). But this essential distinction is not a denial that the Church is also a supernatural community – because of the presence of the Spirit of God. How could anyone find eternal salvation in it, if it was not so!

Jesus and the kingdom

There is a substantial consensus in New Testament scholarship that Jesus' use of the term 'Kingdom of God' means God's active and redemptive sovereign rule. 'Within the symbolic word of the gospels, its main thrust is dynamic strength, even active intervention' (Chilton, 1988, p. 48).[3] 'The biblical nouns refer to the act of ruling' (France, 1990, p. 12). The word means reign, not realm, and refers to actual dynamic power, effective in ministry. Despite much current practice it is misleading to reduce the term to 'kingdom', or to use it as an adjective. The Kingdom of God is God in action as king, restoring his rule through Jesus. Through God's action in Christ 'The Kingdom of God was the hoped-for new age, the eschatological age when God's rule would be fully realized, his people vindicated, and his enemies judged' (Dunn, 1975, p. 47). The basic theological meaning, and the shape of the hope developed in the Old Testament, was that of the new age that would replace the old. But the distinctive feature of Jesus' teaching was that, instead of replacing the old, it had invaded it without totally displacing it. 'Christ has cleft the future in two, and part of it is already present' (Bosch, 1987, pp. 277f.). The kingdom is therefore *The Presence of the Future* (Ladd, 1974). It still awaits its consummation and thus has to be understood as 'already' and 'not yet'.

Understood in this way the Kingdom of God is inseparably and unsurprisingly linked to the people of God. The kingdom was the fulfilment of the story of Israel, not a departure from it. 'Jesus believed that the creator God had purposed from the beginning to deal with the problems within his creation through Israel ... Israel was to be the means through which the world would be saved' (Wright, 2000, p. 19). The kingdom he proclaimed was all encompassing. It was 'the reign of God – God who is creator, upholder and consummator of all that is. We are not talking about one sector of human affairs, one aspect of human life, one strand out of the whole fabric of world history; we are talking about the reign and about the sovereignty of God over all that is, and therefore we are talking about the origin, meaning and end of the universe and of all man's history within the history of the universe' (Newbigin, 1978, p. 32). This understanding of the kingdom sets out the scope and scale of the Church's mission. 'What is mission if not the engagement with God in the entire enterprise of bringing the whole of creation to its intended destiny? A local church cannot claim to be part of this if it only serves itself' (Greenwood, 1996, p. 28).[4]

Above all the reign of God was present in the unique person of Jesus himself. 'Jesus believed that the kingdom was breaking into Israel's history in and through his own presence and work' (Wright, 2000, p. 37). To respond to Jesus was to respond to the kingdom. Jesus' ministry went far beyond the circle of his disciples, and his disciples were called to share in that ministry. But it also included a clear call to discipleship. A Church that serves the kingdom will always be a disciple-making Church.

Sign, instrument and foretaste

Many denominations define the relationship of the Church to the kingdom as sign, instrument or agent, and foretaste.

> The church does more than merely point to a reality beyond itself. By virtue of its participation in the life of God, it is not only a sign and instrument, but also a genuine foretaste of God's Kingdom, called to show forth visibly, in the midst of history, God's final purposes for humankind. (*Mission-shaped Church*, 2004, p. 95)

- *Sign*
  The Church is a sign and disclosure of the Kingdom of God (*Mission-shaped Church*, p. 94). In each locality the Church is to be a clear visible pointer to the Kingdom of God and to Jesus its king. In one sense the Church points away from itself to these greater realities. But in another sense it points to itself as the place where they may be entered and encountered. It is in this sense 'an active sign, an effectual sign of the kingdom' (Cocksworth, 2008, p. 24). 'The Church is the doorway to the Kingdom' (Harper and Metzger, 2009, p. 60).

- *Instrument and agent*
  As the community where the kingdom and the king can most clearly be found, the Church is both an instrument in God's hand – used by him to bring the reality of the kingdom to bear in its locality – and also his agent, his apprentice or junior partner in mission. Lesslie Newbigin argued against describing the Church as the 'agent' of the kingdom because he wished to safeguard the primacy of the Spirit in mission: 'The Church is not so much the agent of the mission, as the locus of the mission. It is God who acts in power by his Spirit' (1989, p. 119). But the term is helpful as long as this distinction is maintained. The Church is called to be God's active partner. 'It is an agent of God's mission proclaiming (through its words), embodying (through its life) and demon-

strating (through its actions) the coming of the Kingdom of God' (Cocksworth, 2008, p. 240).

- *Foretaste*

> The kingdom has created a community that, while not identified with it, is a function of the kingdom's presence and anticipates its consummation at the end of the age. This means that the church is a community both of fulfillment and of hope, realizing the blessings of the future while yet awaiting the fullness of these blessings to be revealed at Christ's second coming. (Harper and Metzger, 2009, p. 48)

It is this understanding of the Church as foretaste of the kingdom that best helps define its missionary task at a time of cultural change. Western, affluent, multi-choice cultures lack hope. The best they have to offer is more of the same, but the Church in each locality is to be a sign of hope, because in its own life and ministry people around it should encounter a foretaste of the future Christ has secured, for that part of his creation within the new heavens and earth. Churches are to be imperfect pilot plants of God's future world.

All local churches exist to preserve, embody and pass on the ancient truths of the faith, but they are to do so as anticipations of the future. 'The relationship between the sojourning Church and the new creation is best understood with the aid of the concept of anticipation' (Volf, 1998, p. 267). If there is to be no poverty in the new heavens and earth, the Church should be seen as a community that cares for the poor. If there is to be no injustice, it is to be seen as a community that challenges injustice. If we will see Christ face to face, then the Church becomes the place where we learn to believe without having seen. If we will enjoy the gracious hospitality of God, the Church must be a place of welcome and hospitality. People should be able to look at a Christian community and, at least, say 'They're certainly not perfect, they're not really my type, and I'm not sure I believe what they believe. But if what they have is half of a glimpse of a believable future, I want to know more.' The fact that these characteristics of the future world are seen among clearly imperfect and flawed people gives hope and an invitation to all, without justifying any wrongdoing.

It is a particular function of the Holy Spirit's ministry to enable the Church to live as such an anticipation: to be the body of Christ for its culture. It is integral to the Holy Spirit's ministry to carry the Church forward in mission in this way.

Church for the kingdom in practice

How then can fresh expressions authentically fulfil the Church's calling to the kingdom? There are good examples whose ministry engages deeply with the poor and the excluded, some of which will be mentioned below. But my purpose is to show more generally, but from actual examples, that good practice in establishing a fresh expression should lead organically to establishing Christian communities with a kingdom orientation. The 'fresh expressions journey' should lead to the planting of communities for the kingdom.

A fresh expressions journey

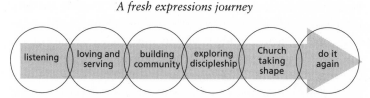

*underpinned by prayer, ongoing listening and
relationship with the wider Church*

An apostolic call lies at the heart of the fresh expressions movement. As the lingering power of Christendom fades, so the Church has to hear the call to go to the great majority, those who no longer come to church or who have never had any connection to it. The Church exists, not for its own sake, but for the place where it is located in the light of God's purposes in Christ. The purpose of a fresh expression is to be a community for networks or parts of a neighbourhood where the Church is not already engaged, in order to fulfil this calling.

'Authentic', a fresh expression of Church in the Glasgow Harbour development. It was established to answer the question 'What does living out God's Kingdom look like for the people of this area?', and to invite residents to 'live a life that is being transformed by a relationship with him ...' (*Expressions*, Ch. 1). King's Cross Church was planted into the area around King's Cross station as it was being redeveloped. It is intended to be a long-term incarnational engagement. 'It's a lot of listening, a lot of pain but ultimately that's the only road to transformation. Our ultimate agenda is to bring new life to King's Cross, to usher in his kingdom' (*Expressions*, Ch. 11).

An apostolic call need not be to a new area. It can be a new way of engaging within the same parish. The congregation of St Luke's, Walthamstow, moved out of their church building to relocate into the weekly Farmer's Market, where they worship and run a fair-trade stall, which is now managed by their priest.[5] In Portsmouth the congregation of St Luke's, Somerstown, also moved out of their church building to establish 'Sunday Sanctuary' in 'the Community Room in Wilmcote House, one of the housing blocks in the area, one where there are lots of young families located and this was a group that we thought the church was not particularly reaching in the whole of the area and particularly obviously in our parish' (*Expressions*, Ch. 23).[6] Wolverhampton Pioneer Ministries, and 'Vitalize', its fresh expression, serve the City's night-time economy and town-centre community, with a particular emphasis on young adults.

We had all these people who were living in Wolverhampton – partying in Wolverhampton – as part of Wolverhampton – who were regularly coming into the city – coming in as groups, as individuals but they were never finding their way into our churches, they were never finding their way into community within the kind of things that church offered. (*Expressions*, Ch. 27)

1 *Listening*

Fresh expressions are birthed in listening to God. They are based on the assumption that the missionary Spirit is at work ahead of the Church, in any place to which he calls his people. Before establishing 'Reconnect' in Poole, Paul Bradbury took time to listen.

> When I arrived we were quite disciplined about spending six months not doing anything. We were new to the area, didn't know anybody, really needed to spend that time praying, prayer walking, listening to what people were saying, speaking to people who knew the community – who had been here quite some time, getting a sense of what God was doing and joining in. (*Expressions*, Ch. 14)

'Streetspace', a fresh expression for young people in Chard, 'is about working with those notions of God and where God is already at with these young people – you're following the *missio dei* – the missionary God – the God who went before us and who we should seek to follow through'(*Expressions*, Ch. 18). In 'Sunday Sanctuary' the move out of the church

> was not to create a service in the tower block that people would come to, but to meet new people – to find out where they were – not to make assumptions about where people were spiritually and in relation to their understanding and experience of faith, but to start from the ground up and make new friends and talk to them and share stories so as to hear their story, as much as to share the stories and the overarching story that we have to share. (*Expressions*, Ch. 23)

2 *Serving*

Developing out of this listening process, fresh expressions begin with service – service that is neither patronizing nor manipulative. It is an end in itself, a little anticipation of the new creation, whatever else may or may not follow. At 'Streetspace' the aim is 'to enhance the personal, social and spiritual development of young people' (*Expressions*, Ch. 18). The leaders of 'Threshold' in Lincoln understand that 'These are people and not projects. If you see planting or starting a church or engaging in a fresh expression as a strategic agenda I think you are doomed from the start – this is God's initiative – it's about his kingdom' (*Expressions*, Ch. 12). The missional communities of St George's, Deal, include 'No Limits', which is creating church among those who are severely disabled, and 'Greenerway', whose focus is the care of the environment (*Expressions*, Ch. 16). An early initiative of 'The Beacon', on a new-built estate near the Dartford Crossing in Kent, was to start a Residents' Association.

> We had an informal meeting in one of the buildings just down the road here, put letters through people's doors and we had about 40 or 50 people come along to that first meeting. And we were very clear that we were a church, that we wanted to work to try and enhance them – to build community here and we wanted to do that firstly by getting residents together in that Association and giving them a voice. We saw that as part of our role of building kingdom really, and part of our witness here as Christians was to ask – in a new community – how do we make it a strong, vibrant and healthy place. (*Expressions*, Ch. 20)

Establishing 'Sunday Sanctuary' has proved to be slow, hard work, but they have achieved 'something the council haven't managed to in their attempts to reach into this particular housing block and to make contact with families and try and help them and support them in their living here' (*Expressions*, Ch. 23). A core aim of Wolverhampton Pioneer Ministries is 'Putting a smile on the face of the city the way Jesus would have done' (*Expressions*, Ch. 27). Fresh expressions of Church are often birthed through a kingdom-oriented ministry.

3 Forming community

These servant ministries, being 'for' the place where God has sent or located them, in the light of the work of Christ, can lead to the establishment of communities that continue and develop that ministry. As new people gather round the founding group, so they see a model of Christian discipleship that expresses itself in such service. Church and kingdom are seen as inseparable.

Fresh expressions like 'Grafted' in Newcastleton (*Expressions*, Ch. 9), 'Zac's Place' in Swansea (*Expressions*, Ch. 28) or 'Streetwise' in Sheffield, each of which focuses their ministry on the poor and marginalized, are seeking to establish healing communities.

> In setting up Streetwise – and in setting up some of our other ministries reaching out to the marginalized – we really genuinely believe if it's going to be effective and make a difference in guys' lives – it needs to be aimed at what they want and where they're coming from. We really want to be a welcoming, inclusive community where people feel that their views can be taken into account – and we really believe that Jesus is good news and that Jesus comes to heal the broken hearted. (*Expressions*, Ch. 19)

For many, belonging has to precede believing; acceptance by the people of God must come before it is possible to understand and receive God' acceptance.

The Methodist Church at Howden Clough was down to seven elderly members, but since it responded to its community's need for a safe place for children and parents to play, by becoming the Wesley Playhouse, it has a new worshipping community as well.

> On Good Friday we had over 100 people here celebrating ... all that it means to be a Christian – 8 different families have asked to have their children baptized in The Playhouse because that's where they've come with their children and

they recognize this as a church – they recognize this is church for them. (*Expressions*, Ch. 24)

Many fresh expressions seek to grow numerically in this way, but some are smaller missional communities whose emphasis is more on their role in the wider community. Mark Berry of 'Safespace' says, 'We've been described as "new friars" I guess – people who come together as a community, develop a rhythm of life and intentional spirituality but the focus is actually what difference do we make to the place we find ourselves in and how are we bringing the kingdom and being agents of the kingdom in the community' (*Expressions*, Ch. 15).

4 Evangelism and disciple-making (Jesus as king)

Whether these are clearly defined groups with a rhythm of life, or more informal networks of new friends, there is often an organic process, where relationships are formed and faith explored simultaneously.

Fresh expressions that are birthed out of service to their locality model a life of discipleship, as do those whose founders have sacrificed their personal, spiritual preferences to plant a community for those with different needs. (*Mission-shaped Church*, p. 30, calls this 'dying to live'.) Evangelism and disciple-making are inseparable. Evangelism calls people to lifelong discipleship, by setting before them a way of life, as a follower of Christ the King.

As it was with Jesus and the Twelve, such disciple-making tends to be primarily through relationships. Sean Stilman of 'Zac's Place' describes is 'an incredibly messy business' (*Expressions*, Ch. 28). But there is no alternative to making a personal and consistent investment in people. Once a fresh expression has developed a regular worship life, this also becomes a resource to shape people in the way of Jesus. Men and women who are exploring the possibility of becoming disciples can explore the reality of discipleship as they join in with programmes of service. For Pete Hughes in King's Cross, 'You actually learn about following Jesus as you serve the poorest of the poor, as you befriend prostitutes, as you befriend drug addicts, the homeless, the working professionals in this area who are on the rat race that London life can be' (*Expressions*, Ch. 11).

A relational approach to mission and discipleship can prove to be a further converting process for founding members of the fresh expression, who find themselves beginning to be changed through it.

5 *Evolving worship*

It is often a mistake to start a fresh expression with a regular public act of worship to which new people are invited. It is not necessarily wrong, but there are two dangers. The first is that the fresh expression is seen as an event to attend, rather than a community of disciples to join. It invites a consumer approach to the Church. Second, the event may be being designed for people with whom there is, as yet, no relationship. It has not been formed with them, for them. The team that developed '3:08@Kingshill' closed it down when they recognized that it was not fulfilling its purpose. 'I suspect that we used the act of worship to build community rather than building community to develop into an act of worship – so I suspect that that was a mistake' (*Expressions*, Ch. 25).

But a worshipping community can emerge through service and a focus on the Kingdom of God and the hospitality of Jesus. 'Zac's Place' is an example.

> I think it's an important milestone when you realize that people are voluntarily coming to gather – not just to receive some food or some clothes – but they are voluntarily gathering to share stories with one another. They're also voluntarily gathering around an open Bible, to learn and there's a desire to learn. They look forward to that opportunity when someone's going to say a prayer, they participate in that, they look forward to taking part in the sacrament of Communion and we've been able to baptize people as well. Those are significant milestones in the process when you realize, actually we've got something here. (*Expressions*, Ch. 28)

A new community, like the 'Beacon', can bear all the authentic marks of the Church.

> Some people want to try and argue that what we're doing isn't really church, it's just an extended house group or something but I really would want to defend what we're doing here by saying that we are authentically church, we are a worshipping community together, we are about God's mission here, we are about demonstrating the Kingdom in this place. We're about worshipping God together and finding ways that are relevant for us to do that. We certainly are creating disciples in what we're doing and encouraging others what it might mean to be a disciple of Christ in this place. (*Expressions*, Ch. 20)

The worship life of a fresh expression need not be minimal, it can be highly creative, as Bishop Michael Perham has shown in *The Hospitality of God*. Worship is transformative and essential to disciple-making. But it must be contextually authentic. Mature fresh expressions will also be eucharistic. A minority of fresh expressions begin with eucharistic worship, but all need to progress towards it, at an appropriate stage of their development as a Christian community.

A test for the whole mixed economy

The continuing challenge facing all churches is to remain missional, to be communities for the kingdom and not revert to the maintenance of their own existence.

> Kingdom agenda and values are often more radical than church readily allows. In bringing the kingdom, God is on the move and the Church is always catching up with him. (*Mission-shaped Church*, p. 86)

The fresh expressions journey creates genuine possibilities for planting communities for the Kingdom of God. But it is easy for any church to lose its original missional edge and kingdom focus (Hardy, 2001, pp. 147f.). Daniel Hardy proposed four dimensions that provide an appropriate health check for any congregation, whether fresh expression or in an inherited mode (Hardy, p. 4).

The first he called *intensification*. To what extent is this community still being formed by the gospel? Is there a deepening and maturing in the faith? (Hardy).

Accompanying this deepening, and as an evidence of it, is *range*. Is there an effective and appropriate contribution to the global issues now confronting the world? The assumption here is that powerful global issues always have local force. Professor Eddie Gibbs has suggested that the marks of any missional church today should include local commitment to global issues. Mission and ministry are 'glocal' (Hardy).

The integrity of this global concern is demonstrated by *affinity* (effectively a synonym for incarnational). Is the ministry of this church 'close enough to the hearts and minds of those to whom they speak' (Hardy)?

The final dimension is *mediation*, which draws all the dimensions together. It involves 'placing the intensity of the gospel in the closest affinity to those lives and societies to which it is addressed' (Hardy).

This vision should be the aspiration of any church that wishes to be a community of the kingdom. It also provokes a longing for the Spirit. To leave the final words to Daniel Hardy, the Church is called 'to participate more fully in the energy of the Spirit of Christ by which God, through his church, is drawing all human society to its fulfilment in the Kingdom of God'.

References

Archbishops' Council, 2004, *Mission-shaped Church*, London: Church House Publishing

David Bosch, 1987, 'Evangelism and Social Transformation', in Vinay Samuel and Christopher Sugden (eds), *The Church in Response to Human Need*, Grand Rapids: Eerdmans

Bruce Chilton and J. I. H. McDonald, 1988, *Jesus and the Ethics of the Kingdom*, Grand Rapids: Eerdmans

Bruce Chilton, 1997, *Pure Kingdom*, London: SPCK

Christopher Cocksworth, 2008, *Holding Together*, London: Canterbury Press

James Dunn, 1975, *Jesus and the Spirit*, London: SCM Press

Expressions: Making a difference, 2011, [DVD], London: Fresh Expressions

R. T. France, 1990, *Divine Government*, London: SPCK

Robin Greenwood, 1996, *Practising Community*, London: SPCK

Brad Harper and Paul Louis Metzger, 2009, *Exploring Ecclesiology*, Grand Rapids: Brazos Press

Daniel W. Hardy, 2001, *Finding the Church*, London: SCM Press

House of Bishops of the General Synod, 1997, *Eucharistic Presidency*, London: Church House Publishing

Hans Kung, 2006, *Why I am a Christian*, London: Continuum

George Eldon Ladd, 1974, *The Presence of the Future*, London: SPCK

Lesslie Newbigin, 1978, *The Open Secret*, London: SPCK

Lesslie Newbigin, 1989, *The Gospel in a Pluralist Society*, London: SPCK

Michael Perham and Mary Gray-Reeves, 2011, *The Hospitality of God*, London: SPCK

Miroslav Volf, 1998, *After Our Likeness*, Grand Rapids: Eerdmans

N. T. Wright, 2000, *The Challenge of Jesus*, London: SPCK

Notes

1 *Mission-shaped Church* is neither a fully developed missiology nor ecclesiology. It is a report on church planting.

2 But see the joint Church of England and Methodist Faith and Order report, 'Fresh Expressions in the Mission of the Church', 2012, London: Church House Publishing, Ch. 5, and Anvil 27 anviljournal.org/index.cfm?p=123

3 See also Bruce D. Chilton, 1997, *Pure Kingdom*, London: SPCK, p. 11 on the language of the kingdom in the Targums (the Aramaic paraphrases of the OT used in the synagogues of Jesus' day).

4 See also *Mission-shaped Church*, p. 85.

5 Fresh Expressions, 2011, *St Luke's in the High Street*, online at: www.freshexpressions.org.uk/node/438 [Accessed 5 March 2012].

6 See also Fresh Expressions, 2011, *Sunday Sanctuary Update Dec '11*, online at: www.freshexpressions.org.uk/stories/sundaysanctuary/update-dec11 [Accessed 9 March 2012].

3

Recovering the Difference
that Makes a Difference:
Fresh Ideas on an Older Theme

RICHARD SUDWORTH

Public worship

One of the main difficulties facing any theological and practical discussion of fresh expressions is that of definition. What
is this beast to which so much energy and so many books are
actually referring? From the proverbial church in a café, pub
and school, to churches that knit, skateboard, contemplate,
travel and search, there seem to be a range of sometimes bewildering venues, interest groups and activities constitutive of
a fresh expression.[1] Reading stories from the fresh expressions
site, it is not always clear at what point an outreach became
church, or a fully formed church just began to shift its location. What is evident, though, is that there is a huge sense of
permission. There is recognition that the Church in Britain
is in a post-Christian context and can no longer assume its
appeal to wider society. Creativity and energy to be present
beyond the traditional boundaries are being encouraged and
displayed. This capacious sense of the inherited Church's reconfigured presence in the emerging culture has come at the
price of some loose self-definition, and this has arguably drawn
the most robust theological critique. In one corner, Davison
and Milbank have criticized the fresh expressions movement
in a bid to reassert the value of the parochial system and the
catholicity of the inherited tradition (2010). In the other corner,

John Hull (2006) has sought to champion the prophetic vocation of the Church in objecting to the apparent consumerism of the originating *Mission-shaped Church* publication (Church Report, 2004).

I would like to suggest a motif that treats these two critiques seriously so as to steer the challenge of mission in the emerging culture while keeping faith with an important legacy of the inherited tradition. This motif, I will argue, provides some self-definition to the creative reimagining of the Church's role in community action, especially when one is attentive to the multi-faith context. It is in that phrase so familiar to Anglicans, but by no means their exclusive preserve, 'public worship', that I see a helpful umbrella for reflection. For the Church of England, there is the classic vocation to be 'cure of souls', every person within a parish having a call on the spiritual care offered by the Church. Each representative minister is likewise very 'publicly' available to and for the surrounding community. Not so long ago, this vocation would be cemented in parishes throughout the country in the central role of the parish church to civic events, such as Remembrance Sunday, and in the pivotal function of the church hall as *the* place of community and social life. The significance of the Church to the universal rites of passage of birth, marriage and death, overlaid and reconstituted in the personal and corporate identity of Christian discipleship, would be normative. All of these ecclesial inheritances speak of our 'public worship' and a presence that is not privatized, or sectarian but, nevertheless, distinctly *Christian* in liturgy and proclamation.

I do not wish to repeat the well-worn material about our post-Christendom context: of the rejection of the Church's narrative or, tellingly, that the Church is not even considered among competing narratives. It is all too clear that the Church is no longer central to local community life in so much of the country. Rather, I would like to posit the shift of post-Christendom as a threat to the ability of the Church, of whatever denomination, to engage in 'public worship'. For me, the vital energy that exists within the Aladdin's cave of fresh expressions stories is where the Church is reimagining what it means to do public worship. This is where the debate about Church and kingdom, radical politics and evangelism, community action and discipleship, comes in.

Andrew Davison and Alison Milbank's *For the Parish* makes a number of heavyweight criticisms of the fresh expressions movement and of the *Mission-shaped Church* document, in particular. One of their foundational arguments is that *Mission-shaped Church* presents an erroneous divide between form and content (see pp. 1–27). They assert that the governing ecclesiology of the fresh expressions movement assumes that the form of Church is extrinsic to the inner reality of any church community. That is, cultural practices can be adopted by churches in mission without altering the essence of what it means to be Church. Thus, sub-cultural groupings may readily become receptacles for church communities because there is a deeper 'spiritual' reality to Church that is unaltered by respective context. This approach ignores the communal and physical nature of faith: following Christ the Lord involves being part of a community of tradition and practice, not just an individualized assent. The argument is sound, though it may be responded that the authors of *Mission-shaped Church* did not have this intention. But by turning the logic back on itself, we arguably highlight the dilemma of mission and the importance of 'public worship'. If, as I would agree, form and content are inextricably intertwined, what does the *form* of the inherited Church tell us about the *content* of the Church of England's gospel? Cynics could be forgiven for answering that this gospel is white, middle-class, middle-aged, literate, introverted and male! As we are committed to a gospel that reconciles cultural, gender, generational, class, and ethnic divides, it means that the Church is evidently failing to be truly 'itself' if the demographic of congregations is so narrow. Davison and Milbank pose a genuine question about the 'form' of the gospel that is encountered in the fresh expressions movement: is there an ecclesiology that goes beyond an individual, conversion experience? But they have failed to provide a way forward for articulating that public faith in contemporary terms. In so doing, they have arguably overlooked examples of mission within the fresh expressions stable that model exactly the 'catholic' spirit they theorize on.

There lies the challenge of mission: to discover a union of form and content that engages, both constructively and abrasively, with wider society in ways that have been lost to the Church. By recognizing the importance of form *as* content, this gospel will be of necessity a holistic one: practical *and* spiritual; personal *and* corporate. Heeding Davison's and Milbank's ecclesiology while creatively engaging our contemporary culture enables us, I believe, to reassert the prophetic edge of the Church that Hull is searching for. What we seek, in fact, is a rediscovery of what *public worship* amounts to today.

The 'ecclesial-turn' in political theology and interfaith relations

Over recent years, there has been a movement in the theology of other faiths away from attempting to provide grand, overarching schema to explain religions.[2] Hitherto, the classic framework has been what is known as the 'threefold typology of religions' that presents perspectives on a spectrum from exclusivist, inclusivist to pluralist. It attempts to provide an outline of views as to the relative truth or value in terms of ultimate destiny for each religion. This schema has fallen into the trap of modernity: of believing that there is an objectively rational standpoint from which to view 'religions'. It amounts to another fissure of form and content: faith being the internal belief system that an individual chooses to agree with rather than a whole corpus of tradition, community and practice. Such an approach subsumes all religions under external categories so that faith itself becomes understood in a way that is probably only correct for one religion.[3] The best and most recent studies are avoiding this 'theology of religions' trap and using as their starting point the self-understanding of the Church. 'Who are *we* and how are *we* to behave?' is the proper preliminary to 'Who are *they*?'[4]

This 'ecclesial-turn' in interfaith relations is also mirrored in political theology.[5] For the likes of Stanley Hauerwas, John

Milbank and Oliver O'Donovan, the Church's role in the public square does not begin with notional, secular ideas of justice or rights but with the preliminary question of 'What is the Church and its role in the world?' This is where I depart from John Hull's critique, which raised the otherwise very valid question about the place of justice and radical politics in the fresh expressions vision. For John Hull, the 'distinction between the Kingdom as a gift and the Church as a human institution' (2006, pp. 4–5) demotes the role of the Church as just one fallible, but admittedly significant, tool for the kingdom. In his reading of the Church, there is a radical disjunction between the Church and the Kingdom of God. There is a danger, then, that Hull is presenting a consequent polarity of attitudes towards other faiths: other-faith majority areas are either envisioned negatively because they are in need of the gospel, as he believes *Mission-shaped Church* does; or positively as partners of *faith*, according to Hull. If the Church is itself a human construct and the kingdom a 'spiritual' entity distinct from it then, of course, all other religions' searches for the divine are on a par with the reductive efforts of the Christian community. The very use of the word 'faith' as an appropriate descriptor beyond a Christian understanding is itself problematic, suggestive of a common cause for those who have a religious sensibility, as if the languages and practices of the religions offered tidy equivalence. Furthermore, the relegation of the role of the Church does little justice to the biblical warrant of Jesus when he confers on the apostles a kingdom (Luke 22.29). It does not do justice to the reciprocal participation in the life of the Trinity that Jesus promises to his community, the Church, after the pattern of his own ministry (John 17). But *neither* does Hull's analysis do justice to the self-understanding of other religious groups who will have different conceptions of 'kingdom', territory, reign and transformation, and may refuse any of our own categories. The important point is that the Church does not *equate* to the kingdom and indeed, from our self-understanding, participating in the Trinity, we will recognize the sovereign act of God's Spirit in the world, beyond the Church, and among other religions. But that work of God's Spirit will be understood in Christian terms and with an appreciation of the Church's eschatological role as the body of Christ: a sacramental divine presence in the world.

The dichotomy, then, between a godless realm of 'other faiths' on the one hand and a coalition of people of faiths around 'kingdom' activities on the other is a false one.[6] Rather, there is a far more nuanced position where the Church is able to work in ad hoc partnership with other communities and traditions where God leads and there are shared objectives, while also presenting the call of the gospel: the challenge of Christ to conversion, baptism and discipleship. There will always be an ontological distinctive, albeit eschatologically, in the Church. The 'body of Christ' proclaims an ultimacy, not to itself, but to Jesus as Lord that cannot but undergird a proclamation to the whole of society. To suggest, as John Hull does, that Christians should be relaxed about the absence of a Christian witness in other faith communities denies the Christian tradition's self-understanding of the Church's unique sacramental role. Hull is rightly concerned about the limited gospel of *Mission-shaped Church* where the possibility of common cause with secular agencies and other faith communities is absent. But my contention would be for a confident concern for mission and the life of the Church across the nation, and among other faiths, in a manner that embodies the good news in integral ways. Such a mission will bring us into partnership, peace-making and dialogue as much as it will produce the fruits of evangelism and discipleship.

Public worship and other faiths[7]

St Christopher's, Springfield, in Birmingham is a Church of England parish church in a Muslim-majority area of the city. In many ways, there is nothing remarkable about the church that might lend itself to be considered as a fresh expression. Yet when visitors see the buzz of activity during weekdays, the dozens of Muslim parents with their children, playing and mixing with congregational members, there is a genuine astonishment at what is seen as an unprecedented place of Christian hospitality.[8]

Through the Springfield Project, the church's community work serving local families with stay-and-play, family support, after-schools clubs and a nursery, St Christopher's has learned a radical reshaping of its vision and developed a very 'public worship' that is making a difference. My contention is that pioneer ministry may be birthed from inherited Church structures, or it may involve a new church plant in a very different form, but that the creative shift that is required is in the fusing of worship, Christian spirituality and practical service in a way that is recognizable to the surrounding community. Christian community action is nothing new: there are swathes of churches throughout the country serving in practical ways and responding to the deepest needs of our society. What is too often lost, though, is the Christian distinctiveness of that practical action. In multi-faith contexts, especially, there is often diffidence about the evident claims of the Christian faith and how these may undermine good relations and the effectiveness of community work.

What St Christopher's has developed is something that does not shy away from owning its inherited story. Christian festivals are acknowledged and celebrated in the project. Prayer is offered to guests coming into the church and project, and working values for staff and volunteers rooted in Bible texts and Christian spirituality. Perhaps the surprise for visitors is that the very public nature of the Christian narrative is *enhancing* the attraction to so many of those belonging to other religious groups. The St Christopher's parish members already know *how to do God* and would prefer to entrust their children to the care of a community with a clear moral compass and a tradition of values and sacred text that has resonances with what is especially important to them than to a sterile, secularized body.

But this 'naming the name' has not been an abrasive and exploitative abuse of the community. Rather, a truly nuanced understanding of God's sacramental presence in the church, and his generous life in the world, has pushed the congregation to places of vulnerability, risk and partnership. As we celebrate Holy Communion, we are proclaiming Christ's lordship: a true union of form and content, in Davison and Milbank's terms. That lordship must somehow be conveyed in the hope of the community project throughout the week. But the manner of that proclamation, of Christ's lordship, will be *cross-shaped*. Thus, seasonal parties for local families will unashamedly acknowledge Christmas and Easter, but no one will be given a 'hard sell' or be invited to anything under false pretences. Staff are given freedom to join with the shared values of the project but to express and affirm how their own, different, religious beliefs can be a source of those values, thus exposing Christians to learning from the other and the possibility of acknowledging what is of God's Spirit beyond the church. The ethics of the community action are equally testimony to the Christian narrative as any naming of the name. The place of Christian community involvement should not be one that perpetuates a dualism between the practical and the spiritual. For those of us working in Muslim contexts, there is the constant challenge to follow Christ without any separation between public and private. In St Christopher's and the Springfield Project, then, there has been an unpredictable journey that has brought Muslims into partnership with the city council, deepened relations with a local mosque, and produced the healthy discomfort that comes with beginning to employ Muslims, Sikhs and Hindus and opening up the volunteer team so that it is now no longer exclusively Christian. A cross-shaped ministry means that the church cannot hold all the cards and engage with the world as an impregnable fortress. Rather, the repeated Christian practices of prayer and worship are to be replayed and reconstituted in the midst of vulnerable change.

The nuanced nature of this approach, where *both* evangelism *and* radical, social action are envisioned, means that the reactions of stakeholders cannot be foreclosed. When the church negotiated the contract to be the largest Children's Centre in Birmingham with the city council, it made clear that it was a congregation that believed in evangelism, yet was committed to good relations, dialogue and peace-making in the Muslim-majority parish. The church was prepared to undermine the expansion of the community work if growth was dependent upon the church losing its confessional edge in the project. Ultimately, the city council *and* the local mosque supported the expansion on those confessional terms because the church was seen to make a practical difference for good *because of* its confessional roots, not despite them.

What St Christopher's has displayed is something of a return to the centrality of the church in the life of a local community. It has done this by taking risks and by focusing a huge amount of its energy of mission into addressing the needs of this surrounding other-faith parish. New partnerships have arisen and new areas of mission been embarked upon. Thus, the consequent interaction across faith groups and burgeoning friendships among staff and volunteers have encouraged the development of intentional activities for interfaith dialogue. 'The Feast' project has been set up, based at the Springfield Project, with a vision to resource dialogue between Christian and Muslim young people in the area with special attention to working in local schools.[9] Again, consonant with the approach of the church's primary project work, these interfaith dialogues do not presume that 'all roads lead to one'; do not offer a bland stew that elides difference. Rather, they offer opportunities for Christians and Muslims to be fully themselves, to disagree, but be friends and build trusting, peace-making friendships through their differences. This is done knowing that there *are* profound similarities between Christians and Muslims and that we often find God speaking to us in the most surprising places and from the most surprising people.

Conclusion

As I write this, I find myself as a newly ordained 'Pioneer Curate' to two neighbouring parishes of St Christopher's. One of these parishes is now without a church building in an area with a significant other-faith majority, and continues as a small worshipping congregation meeting in the church school. We are exploring currently how a community house can become a hub for the existing parish nursing ministry, such that prayer and worship take place in a way much more public and accessible to a community hungry for God's leading. The current Sunday service is prohibitively far from our local neighbours in culture and practical remove. Indeed, the residual mistrust of colonizing, 'Western' Christianity underscores the sort of integral vision displayed by St Christopher's. So any opening up of prayer and worship in that local context must be fused with practical, loving service to be authenticated. There is no doubt that many churches throughout Britain face a particular crisis about their long term viability in inner cities and in areas with significant other-faith populations. Our good news is also good news for Muslims, Sikhs and Hindus and that good news will be found in the community of the church. Without a costly identification with those communities, our worship will remain a privatized affair and will deserve to dwindle. The choice is not between church and mission, because the church is the outflow of the life of the Trinity, expressive of the very character of God and thus inherently missional. We may envision new church plants, meeting at different times and embodying cultural practices that allow the worship to be 'public' to British Asians as Pall Singh's 'Sanctuary' community do.[10] Or a local parish church may venture a degree of partnership that radically shifts its resources and life, as St Christopher's has done. But what the other faiths milieu teaches us is that we can ill afford to bury our Christian distinctive or divorce our practice from our proclamation. As the Victorian theologian F. D. Maurice says, 'the truth of God is not something which we hold, it is something which holds us' (Allchin, 1984, p. 189). That truth continues to call people of all faiths to conversion, but it is a truth that the Church, if poured out in unconditional service, will find echoes of already: the difference that makes the difference.

References

A. M. Allchin, 1984, *The Joy of Creation: An Anglican Meditation on the Place of Mary*, London: Darton, Longman & Todd
Church Report, 2004, *Mission-shaped Church: Church Planting and Fresh Expressions of Church in a Changing Context*, London: Church House Publishing

Andrew Davison and Alison Milbank, 2010, *For the Parish: A Critique of Fresh Expressions*, London: SCM Press
John Hull, 2006, *Mission-shaped Church: A Theological Response*, London: SCM Press

Notes

1 http://www.freshexpressions.org.uk/stories

2 A major text indicative of this move is Michael Barnes' *Theology and the Dialogue of Religions*, 2002, Cambridge: Cambridge University Press.

3 Typically, then, 'salvation' as a Christian term governs our under-standing of the realities of the 'other', dictating what we believe of the Muslim, Hindu or Sikh as if salvation were a concept readily accessible to them. This is not to suggest that the salvation question is not relevant but that it does not give us the key to relating to the 'other' as they would see themselves.

4 An excellent example of this is illustrated by the Anglican Communion's recent document on the theology of relations with other faiths, *Generous Love*: it deliberately shuns any attempt to provide a so-called 'theology of religions' but rather 'begins with God', and thus an under-standing of the Trinity and the nature of Church, and thence how we are to relate to other faiths. *Generous Love* can be downloaded from http://nifcon.anglicancommunion.org/resources/documents/index.cfm

5 Significantly, Andrew Davison also refers to the 'Return to the Church' in the areas of doctrine and biblical theology in 'Theology and the Future of the Church', in Mark Chapman (ed.), *Hope of Things to Come: Anglicanism and the Future*, 2010, London: T&T Clark/Continuum, pp. 69–87.

6 In John Hull's essay 'Mission-shaped and Kingdom focused?' in Stephen Croft (ed.), 2008, *Mission-shaped Questions*, London: Church House Publishing, pp. 114–32, there is a greater attention to the biblical pattern of mission and an important conclusion about the nature of Church as something closer to the sacramental presence of God that I would advocate. It suggests that perhaps the stark dichotomy outlined in *Mission-shaped Church: A Theological Response* may not be representative of Hull's true position. What is recognizable in his concern about the Church's perceived territorial privilege, though, is the need for our mission not to be motivated by self-preservation, and this is perhaps the proper qualification of any comprehensive vision of mission across the nation. Mission is for the good of all people and communities after the manner of God's selfless love for creation, not a bulwark against diminishing congregations, influence and funds.

7 For a fuller account of the contemporary challenge to the Church

of a multi-faith society, see the author's own *Distinctly Welcoming: Christian Presence in a Multifaith Society*, 2007, Bletchley: Scripture Union. A sample chapter from the book on community action, 'Serving with Distinction: Community Action and Other Faiths', can be downloaded from the Community Mission website at: www.communitymission.org.uk/resources/articles_booklets_to_download/default. aspx#serving_distinction. This site has a range of very worthwhile pieces on Christian community action on broader themes.

8 To read more about St Christopher's and other illustrations of church engagements with other faiths, see the author's piece on the Fresh Expressions site, 'Share the Guide': www.sharetheguide.org/examples/faiths

9 See www.thefeast.org.uk/about for details.

10 See www.eastandwest.co.uk/sanctuary.html and www.shareth eguide.org/examples/faiths

4

Death Before Resurrection: Good Friday to Easter Day

PAUL KENNEDY

refresh@winnall

Discernment is at the heart of a life of faith but that doesn't mean we always get it right, and what we are called to today might be different tomorrow. Some plans and projects need to die so that new life can emerge. refresh@winnall is emerging from false starts as well as things that worked for a season: is this a faithful outworking of the need to allow previous projects to die, so that something new can be born; a faith in death before resurrection?

The Winnall estate in Winchester is an area of relative deprivation. It's a long way from the huge estates of urban poverty in other parts of the country but it remains peripheral to the professional culture of Hampshire's county town. There's substantial social housing and the only residential tower blocks in Winchester. A medieval parish church, just off the estate, has struggled to overcome a social and physical dislocation. For a number of years the wider church has struggled to join in with God's mission in this place.

When the parish church was in an interregnum, a fresh expression was established on the estate, drawing on younger people from a large Anglican evangelical church in Winchester. This made good connections with local residents but it petered out when the young people involved moved away to university or new jobs. It was replaced by a Sunday afternoon youth-based fresh expression in the parish church (the parish once again had an ordained priest, the writer, and is now part of the wider East Winchester benefice). This worked for a season, and introduced young people to faith, but it struggled to continue. An adult prayer group then emerged but there was a desire for the prayer group to have a larger vision – one that lovingly engaged with the estate both through serving and sharing faith. refresh@winnall was born.

New birth

Gradually new people came to the prayer group. It met in people's homes with the location shared by text message. Sometimes this was a terraced house, at other times a flat, and occasionally the parish church. People came along who were disenchanted with traditional models of church – whether Anglican or independent – and who wanted a community rooted in the ideas of Acts 2, where goods are held in common and 'they broke bread at home and ate their food with glad and generous hearts, praising God and having the goodwill of all the people' (46–7).

As the prayer group died and was resurrected into a distinctive community, two words became important. First, ekklesia: this was a model of church but not as we previously knew it. For some the very word 'church' had loaded connotations. Second, oikos: we were not suddenly to hold everything in common but this was an emerging household where fellowship and sharing were to be expected. Our kingdom ideals were to be based around serving the estate, sharing the good news and fellowship.

Distinctive roles may emerge, and are recognized as biblical, but there is no one leader, so establishing an ethos could not be easily done in the traditional setting of a chaired meeting. We discussed what needed to be agreed: name, purpose and ethos; we then set up an online document with these headings and a few pointers. Through our meetings and online editing, an agreed document emerged over a few weeks.

We agreed a name, refresh@winnall, showing that location and our context of the estate are important, but also that something new is emerging. It seemed to recall the description of the incarnation in *The Message* Bible: 'The Word became flesh and blood, and moved into the neighborhood' (John 1.14). The purpose refers to being a 'grass roots Christian community', which recalls the desire to be radical (in the sense of rooted) in the experience of the early followers of the way in Acts 2. The ethos covers four areas: 1) community, including sharing our lives and accountability; 2) expectant prayer, both when we meet weekly and personal intercession; 3) discipleship, both as a journey and as specifically recalling the distinctive broken-ness of Jesus on the cross, reflecting the brokenness in the lives of our community and estate; 4) sharing our faith, both with those who journey with us and demonstrated by how we live our lives. refresh has its ethos rooted in kingdom values: com-munity, expectant prayer, discipleship and sharing faith. Over time this ethos may be expressed in a rhythm or rule of life and refresh may resemble a new monastic community. It's early days, but over the last few months we have been fleshing out refresh's vocation.

refresh in the community

We are now developing our ekklesia life and also how we reach out to the wider community. We are an oikos but also an eclec-tic group. We also recognize the need to draw on the experience and gifts of others beyond our geographical community. This is not seeking oversight from another church structure or bishop but a recognition that many have walked similar paths to ours and have much to share.

Two defining passages have been Matthew 10, where the twelve apostles are sent out, and Luke 10, where the seventy are sent. These passages refer to finding the 'person of peace' when we are called into an area. The person of peace is not necessarily a community leader but someone who has some standing within the community, maybe through a circle of friends or contacts. It could be a parent at the school gate or someone who chats at the bar in the community centre. The person of peace can only come to light as we become fully part of the Winnall community: shopping, drinking, walking, visiting school locally.

Peter and Marsha Farmer, who have been involved in small missional communities on estates, came to stay with us for a weekend. Finding the person of peace is key to their understanding of mission. It is an important step to building an ekklesia as the person of peace becomes the focus for any emerging group. They shared a five-stage model:

1 Prayer-walk around the estate: this is intentionally walking the streets and loitering in the public spaces of the estate, asking God to reveal how he is calling us to be involved, and developing an insight in, and compassion for, those who live here.
2 Finding and befriending a person of peace.
3 Enabling a group to develop around the person of peace.
4 The new group develops to become an ekklesia. It is not always clear when this happens but it is likely to be sacramental in some way, breaking bread and baptizing, and also serving the immediate community.
5 The ekklesia reaches a place of independence where oversight is no longer necessary; however it will remain necessary to support the person of peace in their distinctive role within the new ekklesia.

It was an inspiring weekend but it has left as many questions as answers as we discern how to join God in building the kingdom in Winnall. Are we to try and establish micro communities based on local leaders or do we first need to build upon our own fellowship? It has been generally discerned that we need to become more rooted as ekklesia and oikos, and Peter Farmer pointed out that he prayer-walked for nine months with the intention of finding a person of peace before that happened; for Marsha, being a 'school gate mum', this happened far quicker – a women's coffee morning has just taken off there. So we are aiming to become a more intentional community at present, and are moving in a sacramental direction and prayer-walking around the estate. Not so much to find the person of peace at this stage but to become immersed in God's activity in this place: sharing – not a formal Eucharist but an informal meal; planning a contemporary version of a carol service in the community centre, a venture where tea and face-painting will be as important as singing and prayer.

In prayer-walking we have discerned the twin dangers of a dependency culture and apathy. Social provision is needed and plays an important and valuable part in the welfare of many on Winnall. However, a long-term dependence can be built up and carried over into other areas of life if it is relied on over a number of years. refresh could be seen as another branch of welfare and so, instead of empowering the potential person of peace, it would become another support on which they would rely (for example, for company or lifts).

The membership of refresh comes from those who live both on and around the estate, so it is not some well-meaning outside organization. However, our prayer-walking has highlighted the danger of that assumption and the need to be fully integrated into the communities that make up this estate.

refresh and the marks of the kingdom

Are there distinctive marks of the kingdom that particularly resonate within refresh@winnall? The answer should be 'yes' because the context of refresh is distinctive: it does what it says on the tin. The distinctiveness comes both from the personal experience and formation of the members of refresh, and the social context of the Winnall estate.

We did have an initial debate on the idea and place of theology. For some, theological exploration was secondary to 'just getting on with it'. This is an association of theology with introspection but also comes from some church experiences where the professional pastor has laid down a theological understanding and debate has been controlled. Disagreement over theological understandings has been equated with disloyalty and division.

For others, theological reflection was vital. There is an understanding that movements of the 1200s, such as the Franciscans and the Dominicans, are still radical forces within the Church today because their theologians gave them depth and insight, especially Bonaventure and Aquinas. There's also the earlier identification of prayer as theology: 'A theologian is one who prays, and one who prays is a theologian' (Evagrius of Pontus, *c.* 400 CE).

The place of theology was affirmed but so was the style in which this was to be done. Instead of closing debates down so that a 'correct' answer is given, disagreement should be seen as positive and fruitful. In some ways, our theological method is also our ecclesiology. Not having a leader means that you can't disagree with the leader's theological understanding; it is far harder to have a party line.

Two main theological debates have arisen from our context and experience: first, what are we primarily remembering when we remember Jesus; and second, an understanding of the atonement.

How we remember Jesus

The experience of some refresh members of being disenfranchized and hurt by the Church, along with the experience of many on Winnall of being on the margins of society, has informed how we remember Jesus. When we remember him in the breaking of bread it's not because he multiplied bread for the feeding of the 5,000, or because of the other miracles he performed, nor even his teaching. When we break bread to remember Jesus, we are remembering that he was broken. This is a kenotic spirituality recalling how Jesus emptied himself, first of his divine nature in becoming human at the incarnation, and then of human life itself in dying upon the cross (cf. Philippians 2).

'Christ the King' imagery, which relates well to powerful established churches, is rightly subverted to recall the broken Jesus, the lamb who was slain. The kingdom values of Jesus, who emptied himself of divine status, and then touched lepers, honoured tax collectors and spent time with scandalous women, were not about reinforcing contemporary power politics, then or now. They were, and are, about embracing the damaged and walking with the outcast (cf. Matthew 25.31–46). Our theology is our mission and so we are not just about establishing a prayerful community, or communities, on the Winnall estate. We are here to serve and are looking for opportunities for partnership (for example, with the Good Neighbour Scheme), and so our mission primarily takes the form of the kingdom values of love and service, rather than traditional evangelism. Some are also exploring the practice of the Jewish Passover to further understand the Last Supper and our understanding of the sacrifice of the cross.

The atonement

Our second theological emphasis concerns the atonement. Some members of refresh come from a traditional penal substitution understanding. This is the belief that on the cross Jesus paid the price demanded for our sins by the Father. All we have to do is believe this and we are justified before God. Our past sins are no longer held against us as Jesus paid the necessary price to the Father. While this understanding has an attractive simplicity about it, it's also deeply flawed in the assumption that the Father needed to extract punishment from his innocent Son. And we need to believe it to make the mechanics work! Do we want a Father who 'abuses' his Son? And what of all those in post-Christian Winnall who haven't heard and can't comprehend this narrative? Few have shared this narrative in the previous two generations. How should we understand the atonement in our setting from our experience?

Our exploration of the Passover, along with Jesus' brokenness within the Passover context, move us away from a penal substitution understanding of Jesus' self-sacrifice. The lamb killed at the Passover is not slaughtered to appease God but is killed initially as a sign that the household is already reconciled to God, and, in re-enacting the Passover meal, to have a community celebration where God's saving action is made present by being remembered. The lamb is not killed for God, but for us, to initiate our journey and then to be food for that journey.

Within our context two ways of understanding the atonement seem especially appropriate and can only briefly be touched upon here. First, scapegoat theory and the insights of René Girard. Human beings are often drawn to demonize another person or group. For example, our suffering in the recession is the fault of bankers, or benefit scroungers, or immigrants (depending on how you view the world). Then, in your mind, these people need to pay a price because of the damage that they have caused. So if it's bankers who are blamed they can be subject to special tax and regulation; if it's those on benefits, then tough new measures can be introduced; if it's immigrants, then a tightening up of our borders. However, for those who follow Jesus, scapegoating should have died with him on the cross. He took the sacrificial blame for human sin; he is the ultimate and unsurpassable scapegoat, and no further scapegoating should seem appropriate. Jesus reveals the innocence of the sacrificial victim; the guilt of the victim who committed no sin is a lie.

The price that Jesus paid was not to the Father but to us. The hypocrisy of scapegoating has been unveiled. No appropriate price can be paid and the blaming of the scapegoat is an affront to justice. We can stand alongside those who are today's scapegoats, whether it's because they are single parents surviving on benefits or those living with addictive and misunderstood illnesses. Here and now, Winnall, 2011, the scapegoating tools of prejudice, stereotyping and exclusion are anathema to us.

The second way of viewing the atonement draws on the work of the Marxist Slavoj Žižek. For a Marxist, alienation is a human reality and, for Žižek, the ultimate alienation is from the transcendent Father. Luckily, this transcendent understanding of God dies with the incarnation because immanence is achieved in Emmanuel, 'God with us'. However, the pivotal moment for Žižek is over 30 years later at the crucifixion and, specifically, Jesus' cry of 'My God, why hast thou forsaken me?' At this point God ceases to believe in God and, God in an alienated sense, dies. Žižek takes the 'Christian' understanding of the death of God to its conclusion and refers to himself as an atheist. However, he also deduces that the post-resurrection

God then emerges as the social bond within the community as experienced in the Holy Spirit at Pentecost. refresh can be an expression of God's presence on Winnall because alienation from God has been overcome in the atoning work of the incarnation and cross. There are similarities with viewing the Church as the body of Christ; Žižek's view is radically egalitarian, however, and not like some body-of-Christ models of Church, which are used to justify headship and distinctive roles. Following the death of an alienated Father God, Žižek affords no space for a headship hierarchy, which refresh reflects in its desire to avoid traditional models of leadership. However, members of refresh would want to keep an understanding of God as Abba and some refer to Daddy; and so would not adopt in full Žižek's conclusions.

The particular insights that may be gained for the wider Winnall community are that this is an estate alienated from its prosperous neighbours on the other side of the cathedral city. However, we are not called to become like them but to find meaning, purpose and the divine within our own oikos and community. The calling of refresh is not to overcome alienation by mimicking a professional group; it is to call the group to go ever deeper and achieve ekklesia in community involvement.

Conclusion

refresh@winnall has not been established long enough to see if new life has truly been gifted by the death of previous fresh expressions on Winnall. The journey from Good Friday is currently at Holy Saturday evening rather than Easter morning. We have a calling to watch and wait, which can be a struggle for those of us who are activists. For now, quiet community presence is a priority over explicit evangelism.

However, we do have distinctive kingdom values emerging from the tension of past church experience, contextual living and theological reflection. God is perceived as present within the ekklesia of refresh, and the community of Winnall. As the report 'Mission Shaped Church' said, 'It is not the Church of God that has a mission, it is the God of mission that has a

Church.' At Winnall, God also has refresh, where remembering Jesus emptied and broken, and insights from the atonement, help us to listen to the community and the divine. An alienating hierarchical understanding of either God or ekklesia has been replaced by an oikos indwelt by the divine.

5

Operation: Turkey Sandwich

NADIA BOLZ-WEBER

'O my gosh, we're out of turkey', Stuart yells from the kitchen.
The statement puts a quick stop to the action in the church
basement where moments before a clamour of zip-lock baggies,
packets of mayonnaise, pumpkin pie bars and mischievous
holiday cheer seemed unstoppable. Everyone pauses but the
children who, unaware of the work stoppage, continue to
slap 'It sucks you have to work on Thanksgiving. Operation:
Turkey Sandwich, brought to you by House for All Sinners and
Saints' stickers on paper lunch sack after paper lunch sack.

It's our second year doing this: bringing Thanksgiving
lunches to unsuspecting folks all over our city who are unlucky
enough to have to work on a holiday when most of the rest of
us get to be with friends and family. Our sack lunches mirror
the traditional Thanksgiving meal: sandwiches made from
freshly roasted turkeys, pumpkin pie bars and stuffing muf-
fins (all accompanied by salt, pepper, mayonnaise and mustard
packets and a napkin). After assembling the 300 bags, we load
them into our cars and disperse to find any gas-station cashiers,
security guards, bartenders, bus drivers or hospital janitors we
can track down. Hopping out of our cars, we hand them these
little gifts saying 'Sorry you have to work on Thanksgiving!',
jump back in our cars and try and find the next victim. And it's
not just the 'members' of House for All who are involved. The
local newspaper listed OTS as an alternative idea for how to
spend Thanksgiving, and we were inundated with people wanting to participate. So we welcomed so-called strangers into the
life of our church to make some food, assemble some bags and

distribute some joy because the gifts of God are free and for all.

So many people participate in the life of this church besides those who regularly show up to Sunday Eucharist, that it makes the question 'How many people are in your church?' difficult to answer. This church, 'House for All Sinners and Saints', exists in increasingly large concentric circles. While the standard measure of church membership involves who gives money and shows up to liturgy, new missional communities such as ours are living into a more expansive ecclesiology – an ecclesiology that points to what it means to be Church outside of just worship services and committees. Perhaps ironically, the way in which this shift in ecclesiology has happened, at least in our case, is in reclaiming the old idea of a parish. On some level, HFASS is a parish church – our parish is urban Denver and I am a parish pastor. One of the many advantages to not owning a building is that I am never tempted to think that I am justifying my paycheck by the number of hours I am in the church office and available to the members of the congregation (a sad and common reality for a lot of pastors). There is no church office. So I meet people for pastoral care in coffee shops and I sit in local bars and write my sermons. In the last few years I have developed relationships with countless bartenders, shop owners and baristas, resulting in the fact that on some level ... I'm their pastor. They may never say as much since they are not at all 'church folks', but the fact of the matter is that when their mom dies, or when they are in crisis, they come find me. Somehow I have become the person who all the agnostics ask to pray for them. And there in the sacred space of bars and coffee houses we, the children of God who gather as HFASS, are on some very real level, being the Church. And there's nothing we love more than being Church in bars.

Fat Tuesday at the Thin Man

It all started with an Advent prayer service that a couple of the original HFASSers insisted on putting together. It was December of 2007 and I was finally coming home from the semester I was required to spend at Luther Seminary in St Paul Minnesota.

There was, at this point in time, just a group of eight people who were hanging out in my living room once a month getting to know each other while sharing meals and prayer. There really wasn't a whole lot more to it than that. We had no plan, no name, nothing other than some crazy idea that we might want to start a church together. The week before coming home from Luther, two of the eight emailed me to ask if maybe we cold have an Advent prayer service. 'Yeah,' I answered, 'if you put it together. I'm spending that week re-acquainting myself with my husband and kids.' And so they did. Our little group of eight – which were actually only six that night – met in the basement of a bar. At 4 p.m., when we were done chatting and were ready to start our first prayer service, 21 people streamed down the stairs of the Thin Man bar. The two gals who had planned this, our first service, had invited a few friends and the weird thing is, they showed up. We read the genealogy from Matthew's Gospel and we sang. Then Seth played her cello as we asked people to write down what they were waiting for in their own lives, and to clip their papers to the Christmas lights that hung from the ceiling above our heads. We then walked around and read what others had written, and the papers spoke of longings that were beautiful and heartbreaking at the same time. Later that week, when Seth had asked her friends what they thought of the experience, they mentioned how amazing it felt to pray in the basement of a bar, how the space felt sacred and how they realized that there was no where else in their lives where their deepest longings could be voiced and held. To which I responded, 'That's why you need a *church*. When your mom dies, your yoga teacher isn't bringing you a casserole.'

So as we continued to get together each month, then every other week to hang out, eat and pray, we began laughing a lot. I mean *a lot* a lot. There was a very distinct humour in our group that felt like a combination of irreverence, piety, cynicism, silliness and irony. So when we started becoming a more active community, we naturally began to find ways to be who God made us, where God put us. I guess if there is a definition of what it means to be church, this would be it for me: gathering as the people God created us to be, to hear the gospel, receive the sacraments, confess, be absolved and go and do likewise in the place God put us. So before we even had our first Eucharist service we started thinking of ways to be church out in our Denver parish – and since it was late winter we naturally thought: 'We should do Fat Tuesday at the Thin Man!' So on the Tuesday before Ash Wednesday in 2008 we showed up at the Thin Man, a hipster bar in uptown Denver, with six dozen doughnuts, as many blank postcards stamped and already addressed to Post Secret (an internet project where people write their secrets on postcards and send them to someone who curates them into books), along with little sheets of paper containing 40 ideas for keeping a Holy Lent. Then we handed out free doughnuts and postcards all night to folks in the bar, inviting them to *eat up and confess their sins – Lent starts tomorrow*. It was more fun than we ever imagined and the basis for amazing conversations with people we might never have met otherwise. That was perhaps the first time of countless more to come when the question is posed 'Are you guys really a church?' To which we didn't really have a great answer except 'Yeah, we're pretty sure we are.'

Junkies and Maundy Thursday

My friend Jerry, a Los Angeles stand-up comic turned Methodist minister, stands in Civic Center Park every Tuesday and Friday. There among the dishevelled poverty of the inner city he stands with a box of food and a small table on top of which is a loaf of bread and a chalice. 'Hey Steve,' he greets a giant of a man in an old army jacket who carries a backpack as big as his own story, 'can I hook you up with a sandwich? Clean socks? A little communion, buddy; what'll it be?' Jerry's like a Methodist Robin Hood – taking from the rich in his huge suburban parish and giving to the poor in urban Denver. 'I just like to think that I'm getting people who have way too much, to offer some of that to people who have way too little.' The sandwiches he and a few volunteers hand out every week in the park are made during the casual night club-like Sunday evening service Jerry started called After Hours. Every Sunday during After Hours there is a table set up to make sandwiches and assemble bags for Jerry to take to the park that week. Serving is part of that community's worship life.

In the early spring of 2009, as a group of HFASSers met to discuss our first Holy Week together, we spoke of Maundy Thursday and the tradition of foot washing. We spoke of how really, when it comes right down to it, God meets us with dirty feet, not just when we ourselves manage to clean them up. God was made human and walked among us – walked among the despised and wretched, the rich and haughty – and did so – does so – when we are unclean. The love of God comes to us not when we've managed to clean ourselves up a bit; not when God is good and sure that we believe all the right doctrine. God meets us here, now, when our feet are dirty. He kneels before us in love and says: Here's what I'm about. Here's the only doctrine you need ... God pouring out God's self and saying now you do the same ... don't be ashamed of your dirty feet because I will touch them ... I will change you.

This following Jesus thing is not a kind of personal dirt management programme, which is what it feels like the Church has so often been about. Rather than living into the discomforting and radical reality that God loves us dirt and all, the Church has chosen to make the life of faith about worthiness. We're like, experts in this. Only those who are worthy may receive Christ at communion – you have to be baptized (or baptized in the right church), or you need to have confessed first, or agree with our really pure doctrine. Basically, you must have thoroughly cleaned your own feet before sitting at Jesus' table. But we miss the point when we try managing our stuff in order to be worthy of being in Christ's presence. I guess I wonder if a guy who is willing to take off his cloak, wrap the towel of a servant girl around him and wash the filthy feet of his friends who are about to betray him is a guy who would start a religion based on the shame and worthiness of those he loves. He asked nothing of them but to love each other, dirt and all. After all, the dirt is inevitable and not the result of anything but our journey as the broken. To not have the dirt is to not have been on the road at all. Dirt is simply the inevitable experience of being on the road. Yes, we too need to be washed of the buildup of being simply ourselves in the world. It comes off not because we are worthy or have managed to gussy ourselves up for Jesus, but because he has done something to us. He has come to us while our feet are still dirty and said, 'Let me take care of that.' He commands us to love in this same crazy way.

So, inspired by After Hours, we came up with the idea of including two activities during the foot-washing time in the Maundy Thursday liturgy. We took turns washing each other's feet; but also we stood at a table overflowing with condoms, bleach, cotton balls, tourniquets and cookers – we sang 'Take O Take Me As I Am' while assembling bleach kits for the Denver needle exchange. The liturgy, the work of the people, that evening included the assembly of kits to be distributed by outreach workers so that intravenous drug users on the streets of Denver could clean their needles and practise safer drug use. Because God meets us with dirty feet. All of us.

The blessing of the bicycles

Urban biking is not without peril. Many of my parishioners rely almost exclusively on human-powered transportation, and do so while competing for road space with motorized vehicles. As a way of acknowledging the inherent goodness of God's gifts of life and health and the humble but elegant bicycle, we decided to conduct a Blessing of the Bicycles for the entire Denver cycling community. This event was open to all, regardless of religious affiliation, race, creed, colour, sexual orientation, fat or thin tires, and brand of bike. We even welcome unicyclists and Unitarians. Some may have taken it more seriously than others but it doesn't matter. As we swung our homemade thurible (made by a friend of the community entirely from vintage bike parts) of incense over the Schwinns and Cannondales, we did so as a human community seeking God's blessing and protection for all who brave our city streets on two wheels.

Here are our prayers, which we wrote the day before and have now been purchased by Augsburg Fortress (the Lutheran publishing house) and added to the list of worship ideas on their website.

Present in a world groaning under the excesses of consumption, we acknowledge the inherent goodness of non-motorized human-powered transportation and give thanks for the simple beauty of the bicycle. God of life,
Hear our prayer.

Present in a community filled with children, we pray for those learning to ride. Keep them smart, safe, and visible on their neighborhood roads. God of life,
Hear our prayer.

Present in a community filled with strife, we pray for the victims of road rage and bike theft. And we ask for the strength to forgive mean people. God of life,
Hear our prayer.

Present in a world of work, we pray for those who build, repair, and clean our bikes and those who rely on bicycles to earn their living. Bless those who choose to not drive to work and those for whom driving isn't even an option. God of life,
Hear our prayer.

Present in a community of beautiful diversity, we ask your protection and blessing on all who ride: pedi-cabbies, weekend warriors, athletes, homeless folks, students, children, eco-warriors, bike co-op anarchists, messengers, and all the others who take to the Denver streets, bike paths, parks, and mountains. Keep us safe as we ride. God of life,
Hear our prayer.

We now observe a moment of silence for all who have died while riding ...
God of life,
Hear our prayer.

AMEN

I write these final few pages having just come home from our community's Theology Pub. Every month we gather in the Horseshoe Lounge to talk theology. So many people show up to this event that we have to break up into two, sometimes three groups. Talking about forgiveness, last night's topic, over 80s pop music, my group consisted of four HFASSers, one United Church of Christ, one Roman Catholic and a couple of Evangelicals. We shared our experiences, talked about the meaning of reconciliation, reminded each other of the cross, disagreed about free will and knocked back a couple of beers. That is to say, we were being church.

As I was leaving, the young Roman Catholic man who had joined us for the first time thanked me for creating a space where our conversation could take place. Is he going to 'join our church'? There are two answers to that: 1) no; 2) he already has. You see, when we started doing all these things out in the community and were joined by so many people (like last Friday when there were 60 people at Beer & Carols – only 18 of whom were actually HFASS 'members'), I thought that these fun, quirky events would draw lots of new people into our regular Sunday worshipping community. That never happened. Ends up, that's been a lousy church growth strategy. And for a few months early on I even began to actually believe that these events were a failure. Then, like so often is the case when you are part of this whole death-and-resurrection thing called Christianity, I realized that I had been seeing it all wrong. I think we call this repentance. These events are an end – not a *means* to an end. We live out our life as a church in public, porous ways in which others are always invited to participate, and they do. The point is not to get them to join us on Sundays for the Eucharist. The point is that the Eucharist sustains us in the life we live out all week long, in which so many others participate.

6

Changes and a Changeless Faith

PHYLLIS TICKLE

Christianity was scarcely out of diapers and into knickers before it began evidencing an obsessive concern with two issues. Both of them were basically existential, at least in a manner of speaking, and both have continued to plague the faith on a recurring, relentless and alternating basis. The first of them has to do with the nature of God and the second with the nature of Jesus, the Messiah. Literally hundreds of thousands of human beings, cumulatively, have died as a result of warfare over the resulting confusion and overwrought passion caused by this deadly duo.

The first to raise its head was the question about the nature of God. Or more specifically: if there was indeed a Trinity, as Scripture seemed to indicate, then what would a triune deity be? How is such even to be understood? Are we to understand that there are three parts to God? Or is God one, but presents as three agencies or modes of operation? Are all the parts equal? Are they co-eternal? Are they a congress of their parts or are they one part in concert as are the colours in a fire when it burns high? And so on.

The permutations and subtleties are almost as limitless as they have proved to be deadly. Not only did Christians go for the throat of other and differing Christians, but communion after communion rose up in aggregate to quarrel viciously and destructively over the orthodoxy of their particular position. Most famously, of course, the strife led to the Great Schism of the eleventh century and to the final severance of Western or Latin Christianity from Eastern or Orthodox Christianity. (It is also fair to say that Christian confusion about one-god-in-three-parts and how that might work facilitated, in many ways, the birthing and growth of Islam. The near-eastern peoples who shared the same land mass with early Christians found the incipient polytheism inherent in such Christian arguments to be a distinct threat to their fiercely monotheistic region and cultures.)

The second question, while it first surfaced a century or so after the nature-of-God question, came to a high and heady boil more rapidly. By the middle of the fifth century, churchman was indeed going after churchman and communion after communion with a vigour and tenacity from which the Church Universal has never entirely recovered. The Council of Chalcedon in 451 CE and the councils that followed it in the sixth century and thereafter were hardly more than opening salvos for an ongoing and still unresolved debate. Is/was Jesus completely and/or always divine? Or was he simply a human being into whom God infused godness at some point, probably at his baptism? Or, instead, was he of two natures – one human and one divine – sharing a common substance within time? Or perhaps he was of two substances within one biography and capable of experiencing and operating both simultaneously? Looked at from another, but closely related angle, how was one to understand the Virgin if one could not understand the Son? Was the Virgin to be understood as having borne God? Or just a man-child? Or both? Or none of the above until after the fact? And so on.

And thus it has gone for two thousand years. In times of cultural stress and upheaval, one or the other of the two questions will plague an era of Church history and then, in due time, will step back so that the other may step forward and re-assume its place as the pivotal concern in other new and equally pivotal times.

We are, admittedly, a bit more cautious nowadays than our forebears were about physical engagement with our two historic questions; but becoming less physical in our means of disagreement over the last two or three centuries has neither beggared the questions nor lulled our unresolved tensions.

Rather, our lack of common doctrinal understanding about one or the other of the two has simply managed to hum along as a kind of chronic, annoying discontent; until fairly recently, when once more our lack of uniform clarity morphed into an insistent and undeniable pain demanding to be wrestled with. Simply put, what that means is that just as the sixth century and the eleventh century and the sixteenth century were times of great social and religious upheaval, so also is this twenty-first century in which we find ourselves. Like those previous eras of massive change, we too are facing ancient quandaries from within a new context.

Whether one chooses to speak of Western culture or first-world culture or, more accurately, of those parts of the world that practise Latin or Latinized Christianity, the truth is that the cultures and societies that are so denoted pass, about every half a millennium, through times of major upheaval. Every aspect of their common life, be it economic, political, intellectual or sociological, undergoes massive restructuring; and that storm of pervasive change always involves, as well, a re-structuring of the forms of religion(s) that hold hegemony at the time of shift. We are in such a time now.

The upheaval or tsunami we are passing through in the twenty-first century is the Great Emergence; and just as the Great Reformation of five hundred years ago gave us the rise of the nation-state, the birth of capitalism, the growth of the middle class and, oh! by the way, Protestant Christianity, so the Great Emergence is giving us Thomas Friedman's 'flat world' and the globalization of its cultures, the 'mergonomics' of the world's economies, the non-nuclear and/or extended family as a norm, the ascendancy of information and technology as the basis of barter and, oh! by the way, Emergence Christianity (not to mention Emergence Judaism as well).[1]

Like its most immediate sibling of Protestantism, Emergence Christianity is composed of many member parts. If Protestantism presents in real life as Baptists and Presbyterians and Lutherans and Methodists and Evangelicals and so on, so Emergence presents in real life as emergings, emergents, missionals, neo-monastics, hyphenateds, fresh expressions among others

And as was the case with Protestantism, so it is with Emergence. All the member-parts may be distinguishable one from another, but they are all held together and seen as belonging together, because they all share with one another a basic set of sensibilities, a similar world view or context, and a common mode or timbre of conversation. They all are (and know themselves to be) kindred member-parts of a new form of Christianity that is being born now and here in the same way that Protestantism was born from within Roman Catholicism five hundred years ago.

When we set out, then, to discuss so central and substantial an issue as fresh expressions and the Kingdom of God, we must be quite sure that we are engaging all the named parts of that issue within the context out of which they have come to us and also from the context in which they see themselves as functioning. Thus, the Kingdom of God can hardly be discussed without some prior discussion of what we currently mean to denote by 'God' and/or by 'kingdom'. In similar fashion, we must arrive at some shared understanding of 'fresh expressions' as a definable entity, if we are to juxtapose that concept with the other two of God and kingdom.

For the purposes of economy of effort, if not of academic precision, we can define fresh expressions as a member-part or presentation of Emergence Christianity that occurs principally in those parts of the world for which English has been the primary language (the United Kingdom, Ireland, Australia, New Zealand, Canada and the United States) and in whose ecclesial history and praxis the Church of England has served as forebear and/or informing influence. The term 'fresh expressions' itself has an alter ego or linguistic twin, 'anglimergence'. If one wishes to be an absolute purist about the matter, then anglimergence seeks to name that form of Christian thought and worship that is characteristic of fresh expressions groups. In reality, the two terms tend to be used interchangeably, especially in the United States where anglimergence is routinely used to name both the body of thought itself as well as the groups practising it.

Either way, whether one speaks of anglimergence and anglimergents or of fresh expressions of Church, one is still referring to an entity that is the quintessential embodiment of a major facet of Emergence Christianity. That is, by whichever name they may be called, anglimergence and fresh expressions have been born out of the pervasive and abiding distrust and suspicion in our times of any institution, regardless of whether that institution be social or political or religious.

When Dietrich Bonhoeffer spoke, decades ago, about religionless Christianity, he may have intended – and probably did – something other than what is forming among us now, but that does not make him any the less prescient or his term any the less applicable. Emergence Christianity, like every other part of Great Emergence society, is deeply persuaded that the institution – any institution – by its very nature must strive to preserve and further itself. It therefore follows that the institution – any institution – will always argue passionately and often monomaniacly that the greater good is only served by its own continuation at all costs. Emergence Christians, like Emergence society, will argue, on the other hand, that it is the community that takes precedence, the gathered community out of which direction and order must come, the community in concert is where authority lies, except ...

Except that, even sharing that more general suspicion of institutions, some Emergence Christians suspect as well the tyranny of the group, the risk of error inherent in unfettered immediacy, the lack of economy patent in having constantly to reinvent all the courses of life. Those who share these reservations and who wish to find some common ground between the suspect institution and the vitality of the autonomous community are hybrids and usually call themselves by the hyphenated names of Presbymergents, Methomergents, Luthermergents and so on, according to their natal persuasions. Of these, anglimergents or fresh expressions are one of – and perhaps already 'the' – largest subsets.

It is because of this mixed loyalty that anglimergent Christians, through fresh expressions, seek to create worshipping, serving communities that reverence the aesthetic and experience of the institution without compromising the autonomy of the group. Such would be a tricky business in the best of times.

It is certainly made no easier in our times by the fact that in several important places the theology of the institution – that is, of the Anglican tradition – is no longer entirely congruent with the theology of Emergence Christianity, hyphenated or otherwise; which, of course, gets us back to the business of God and of the kingdom.

If one of the principal hallmarks of the Great Emergence is distrust of institutions, then just as surely an increasingly more Orthodox understanding of the Trinity is likewise a principal hallmark of Emergence Christianity in all its presentations. One of the most frequently noted characteristics of Emergence Christianity, in fact, is its natural affinity for, and inclination towards, all things Anglican and/or Orthodox as opposed to things Roman and/or Protestant; and in the matter of the Trinity, that natural inclination is distinctively bent towards Orthodoxy. That is to say that Emergence Christianity is far nearer to the position of a co-eternal, co-equal triune, indivisible Godhead than, in all probability, is any other form of Western Christianity in the twenty-first century.

While most modern Western Christians would cringe if they were forced to say so publicly, the truth is that both Protestantism and Roman Catholicism have given rise, over the last five hundred to a thousand years, to a body of believers who fathomed – or at least felt that they fathomed – God the Father. There is a clear human analogue, and we were pleased to apply it, however inadequate and eventually dangerous that shortcut may prove to have been. Then there was God the Son, who also stood solidly within known familial structures and whom, therefore, the faithful were comfortable in seeing as part of the Godhead. That relationship and the familiarity of it managed to fend off some of those earlier questions about who came from whom, or if one came from the other, or just how all of that worked. Father and Son as known concepts could be used as a kind of bridge across the difficulties, if one were quick-tongued enough. It was the Spirit that was troublesome.

First of all, there was no fortuitous human analogue for the Spirit. Or at least the analogues there were, were not familial and therefore, when applied to understanding the Spirit, were not also equally applicable to the Father and the Son. The result was that the Spirit got set aside whenever possible, and/ or relegated to the realm of the 'spooky unknown'. This way of dealing with the third part of the Trinity was enabled by the fact that one could argue that the Holy Spirit had not been corporately visible or visibly active in a generalized way since Pentecost and shortly thereafter, seemingly preferring instead to present and work on a much smaller scale of particular individuals or in particular places. There were exceptions to this fairly sanguine approach, of course, especially in the latter part of the nineteenth century, but they were usually explained away as the function of mass hysteria or as a regrettable susceptibility to suggestion born of ignorance among the ignorant. With the coming of the twentieth century, that all changed, and dramatically so.

Whatever one may say of Azusa Street and of the coming of the Spirit upon those gathered there, nothing changes the fact that in 1906 Pentecostalism was born in that place and among those people. Western Christianity was changed forever (as would seem appropriate, we might note) in an old livery stable, so much so that Pentecostalism is presently Christianity's fastest growing component. More importantly, perhaps, the way was opened for the vibrant trinitarianism of Emergence Christianity. And beyond all that, Christian praxis itself was also most assuredly changed.

For the first time in centuries, there were no barriers in Christian worship. On Azusa and among the burgeoning congregations springing out from it, for the first time in almost two thousand years, all people were welcome as equal participants. Both women and men could speak and testify and preach. The wealthy were no different from the poor, for all received the gifts of the Spirit equally. All the races, too, were equal before the Spirit. Be they Native American, African-American, Caucasian-American, Asian-American, Latin-American, it made no difference. All that mattered was whether or not the Spirit was speaking to and through them. The overarching concept of Emergence and/or hyphenated praxis had been born.

But something else, too, had been born. The Age of the

Spirit had come, just as many of the mystics had promised it would. Authority now rested not only in Scripture, as Luther and Protestantism had argued, but also in the intentions of the Spirit as they were revealed to, and discerned by, the devout in prayer and in congress with one another. It was a shift of historic proportions.

Whereas for the first few centuries, Christians had found their roots and stability in the presence of those who had known Jesus, or who had known those who had known Jesus, or who had known those who had known those who had known Jesus, later centuries could not enjoy the comfort of such familiarity. When, inevitably, informed and pseudo-direct testimony was no longer either present or creditable, the Church, of necessity, had to turn elsewhere, and it turned to the business of belief. Creeds and doctrine and dogma became the attested definitions of what 'Christian' was. There is a patent absurdity, of course, in thinking that Christianity (or any other religion, for that matter) can be contained and all its workings plumbed by human logic and intellect; but the system of dogma, doctrine and creed managed to persuade the faithful for centuries. They persuaded with varying degrees of success, that is, until Azusa Street.

What spread throughout the twentieth century from Azusa Street to both cover the globe and also become a major component of Emergence Christianity was not just Pentecostalism as a distinct way of practising Christianity. What spread also was the charismatic attitude or understanding or sensibility that undergirds Pentecostal practice. What spread was the acceptance of discernment as an ordinary, everyday, available-to-any-and-every-prayerful-believer means of direct and two-way contact between the creature and the Creator. Revelations, both individual and within the praying community, are to be expected. 'Of course, the Spirit speaks! Why ever would the Spirit not speak to us directly as well as through Scripture?' asks the Emergence Christian, regardless of what stripe he or she may be.

Out of this cataclysmic change in direct communal and individual intercourse with the Spirit has come the obvious redefinition of just where authority lies or may ultimately be shown to lie for the faithful of the coming centuries. Almost as significant, however, may be the fact that there is a radical trinitarianism underlying and informing it all. The believing community is now understood as bound to one another by the sharing and ministrations of the Spirit as surely as all its pieces and parts traditionally were seen as bound by participation in the Eucharist. In fact, many Emergence believers would find it strange that someone might see a value difference between those two bindings, for each is witness to and integral to the other. Godhead is Godhead, a dance (*perichoresis*, the Greek word for dance, is frequently used here) of mystery and the overwhelming, overarching beauty in which we participate.

The results of such trinitarianism are too numerous to explore now, even as more are just beginning to make themselves evident. Not only does the community have a new configuration and set of connecting sinews, not only does authority now rest firmly in discernment of both Scripture and direct engagement, not only is God infinitely immediate and intimately omnipresent, but the old bug-a-boo question of Christology, because of these changes, has come to be seen as falling somewhere between outright silliness and pure sophistry. As a consummation, such is devoutly to be desired, to quote the poet ... at least for now. But what of the kingdom?

Perhaps the most dramatic change is in the conceptualizations of 'kingdom' that have entered the conversation with the coming of Emergence – changes, if you will, in how 'kingdom' itself is to be understood or envisioned. If God is a *perichoresis* that dances in us and through us and with us, then the dance is not about us. It is about the Whole, about some mystery that is palpable but not subject to dissection or even to naming. It is not about any particular one of us as separate from, or independent of, any of the rest of us. It is all of us in aggregate, for none of us *is* in any other way than in aggregate. It is the dance, and we are both the dancers and the music.

Within this understanding, then, only radical obedience, like radical trinitarianism, makes sense. To not lose all for the sake of this *perichoresis* is to be unworthy of it, just as we were told by Jesus two thousand years ago. Nor is the kingdom some kind of top-down, political structure. Such, Emergence says, is indeed the false imaging that has strangled the faith and the faithful for long enough. No, the kingdom is a lace-work of inter-connected and equi-connected nodes or pods, like a spider's web that vibrates when any one of its strands is touched ... like the internet when any one of its sites makes contact with millions of other nodes, and reality is changed thereby. The kingdom is horizontal not hierarchical, and it is here, and it is now.

Because of these new definitions, the business of being Christian is construed by Emergence as considerably less individualistic than previously was the case, especially than has been the case in the centuries since the coming of Protestant-ism. More significantly, because of the new definitions, an abiding and vigorous concern for the wellbeing of all peoples has been a major hallmark of Emergence. To refer to this dominant characteristic as being a dedication to 'social justice' is almost to obscure the thing being talked about, however.

Social justice is a political term – or, at the very least, a politi-cized one – that argues as frequently for equality and humane concern on the basis of civic common sense as it does on the basis of Christian or religious obligation and duty. Emergence Christianity argues neither of those things. It argues instead the oneness of the dance and the wholeness of God within which we exist. This confusion of secular with sacred motivation has given rise to one of the most charming (or, at least, most affect-ing) expressions of recent times.

When one goes as part of a team to build a house for the homeless or to work a soup kitchen or a food pantry for the hungry, one has done a very sensible thing, a good and benefi-cial thing, in fact. But what one has done may be, in reality, an act of 'inhumane kindness'. That is, Emergence would argue, so long as 'we' did that for 'them' – or, worse, 'I' built that or served that for 'them' – we have not engaged in holy oneness. Rather, we have acted out of the I/them or us/them mind-set that is the chasm between morally laudable action and a one-in-Christ action that unites both pieces of a fair exchange.

In the same way that 'kingdom' is no longer conceptualized as a top-down hierarchy, in the same way that acts of human care are no longer to be construed as acts primarily of Christian obligation, and in the same way that neither heaven nor the Kingdom of God can be engaged any longer as individual goals and rewards, so too can the position of the kingdom no longer be understood as existing in the sweet bye-and-bye. (Truth told, of course, the 'no longer' part of that formula is almost ludicrous. Jesus himself argued over and over again that the kingdom, be it of God or of heaven, was already among, and in the midst of, his hearers; that it was indeed within them; that it was both present and coming.) It is a kind of reversed literalism – a not infrequent component of Emergence thought – that has Emergence Christians now taking very literally what modern and earlier Christians had often chosen to regard as metaphor or, even worse, as oratorical hyperbole.

A kingdom positioned in the here and the now is one part of Emergence understanding of that kingdom and of how Christian participation in it is to be conducted. Another part – and one that is perhaps even more often cited by Emergence Christians themselves – lies in the opening and concluding books of the Bible, as well as some pregnant words that occur between those two. That is to say, Emergence Christians are passionately 'green'; but as with the catchphrase of social justice, so with the catch label of green. Being green in one's politics and decision-making is basic common sense, but it also currently enjoys a kind of moral status or social and political re-enforcement that occludes the reason for green-ness among Christians. Rather, an Emergence Christian is informed by the theses of Genesis and the images of the Revelation of St John.

God made the earth and all things in it; he declared them good and very good. He handed them over to human keeping, telling our forebears to go forth and occupy the earth, tend it, care for it and for the creatures on it. To not tend the earth is, therefore, a direct, if careless, sin. As a sin, however, it has its greatest significance not as a lazy lapse in obedience, but as a violation of the oft-stated plan of a not-yet-complete creation that is still a-borning.

It is on earth as well as heaven that God's will, in due time, will come to be done. It is to the earth that the City of God, in the end, will descend and with unspeakable grandeur occupy the earth, the space between that City and heaven coming to be no more than a continuation, one of the other. And, beyond all possibility of misinterpretation, there are always the Master's words that the kingdom is here, not there, now as well as then. Every act that violates that sanctity violates the Covenant. And as a result of such thinking, every daily and ordinary act is a missional act, and all missions become home missions, whether at Starbuck's or the nearest pub.

To assume, of course, that any brief overview like this one could even name, much less adequately cover, the whole panoply of convictions and topics present in the Emergence conversation just now would be ludicrous. Rather, our purpose here is to hold up for thoughtful consideration those few strands of the larger conversation that appear to have the greatest likelihood of effecting and/or informing fresh expressions Christians as they live their faith as hyphenateds within the Kingdom of God.

Like all hyphenated Emergence Christians and as is patent in their name, fresh expressions Christians are fully shaped by the Great Emergence, its attitudes and principles, values and definitions. (By and large, most of us alive today in the Great Emergence cannot escape it either, short of retreating to an ice floe somewhere, and even that would be tenuous. What is meant here by 'fully', then, is more a matter of degree than anything else.)

But being shaped and imbued with the overall contours and sensibilities of Emergence is not to say, for hyphenateds at least, that all that has been must now be abandoned; quite the contrary. For fresh expressions Christians, as for all hyphenateds, there is not only much in traditional Church that can and should be saved from discard, but there is also much that fits quite cleanly and precisely within the needs and sensibilities of Emergence Christian practice and worship. Indeed, there is much in traditional or inherited Church that, for hyphenateds, is absolutely essential to any type of – and, most particularly, to any Emergence forms of – Christian worship and praxis as those things relate to the Kingdom of God.

We have already noted an affinity, both in theology and in aesthetics, between Emergence Christianity and Orthodox and Anglican expressions of the faith. There are several reasons for this, principal among them, perhaps, being the fact that in both of these older bodies, the Church of Mystery has always trumped the Church of Rules, a modus operandi that is completely sympathetic to Emergence thought. Beyond that, there is, rampant in Emergence Christianity, an almost insatiable longing for what the late Robert Weber, in the early 1970s, named 'the ancient future'. What Weber was noting and naming for the first time is the current hunger to jump fifteen hundred or two thousand years of human manipulation and political dogmatizing in order to get back to Jesus of Nazareth, to the passion and clarity of early believers and to the purity of affection and awe that were original Christian worship.

No one, not even the most naive among us, really thinks such a goal is achievable. As an objection, however, feasibility has rarely been either a satisfaction or a deterrent to the impassioned. Protestantism, in many ways, is seen then as the form of Christianity that Emergence is presently most actively questioning or pushing back from. Roman Catholicism, for its part, is the form of Church that, at least on the surface of things, is responsible for most of the cumulative stultifying of the faith, not to mention the fact that it has also managed over the centuries to become the most hierarchical and inflexible form of the faith. It follows by default that Anglicanism and Orthodoxy are left as the most cordial points of connection with what once was and what, for Emergence Christians, must be again. Whether all of this is defensible factually is not the point. The point is that such is the perception. The point also is that Anglicanism is, for reasons of language and familiarity, if nothing else, the more accessible and compatible of the two standing parties. This means a number of things, no doubt, but two are of prime importance here.

First, it means that fresh expressions and/or anglimergence may reasonably be expected to become the largest subgroup among the hyphenateds and one of the more influential ones within Emergence Christianity itself. Second, it means that established Anglicanism must understand today, if not yesterday, that our prayers and energies and resources are going to have to be spent without restraint or parsimony or self-interest in the business of seeing that fresh expressions thrive and flourish. The treasures of Anglicanism were never ours, of course, though we have often been pleased to think so. They are instead the treasures of the faith deposited into our history for safekeeping until just such a time as this. Now they are ours to give up or offer up or disburse not just to our anglimergence co-religionists, but also, and perhaps more importantly, through them to Emergence Christians wherever they may chance to be.

Again, it was Robert Weber who, in the late 1960s, coined the bon mot, 'Evangelicals on the Canterbury Trail'. With that turn of phrase, Weber was recognizing, quite correctly in fact, that the groundswell of movement towards Anglican spirituality and liturgical praxis had already begun. His only error was in not realizing at the time that what he was seeing on the Canterbury Trail was Emergence Christianity rather than just some variant, or new, form of Evangelicalism. By whatever name, however, Weber's migration was, in large part, a migration towards liturgy and Celtic spirituality and – to call it by its larger name – towards transcendence.

Emergence Christianity is wary of real estate and, in particular, of owning any of it. For a group to own a piece of property is, almost immediately, to have to appoint a caretaker or overseer or responsible party who will, in time, himself or herself require help and oversight, which help and oversight will themselves in time require organizing, who will in time … And, says Emergence, then we are back to hierarchy, to vestries and parish councils and ultimately to dioceses and so on, ad infinitum.

Better, say most Emergence Christians, to borrow space, or use domestic space for worship, or rent already distressed space with no upkeep expectations and minimal liability. Except, of course, there is a problem. None of the above is sacred space. True, each of them may be adorned or furbished with sacred objects and symbols, just as they may be polished with the affection and fervour and prayers of those who gather there; but such spaces, by virtue of their very transitoriness, if nothing else, can almost never achieve grandeur or the whispering prayers and hopes of the ages or the teaching impact of sacred architectural art. That is, while such places are very compatible to Emergence sensibilities and lifestyle, they lack transcendence. They can be part of the mix; in fact, they are much the larger part of it, but they cannot be all of it. There must be both spaces and practices that bind the interior soul, as if by wired connection or opened conduit, directly and affectingly with the Holy as it has been known and followed and enjoyed and adored through all the ages since time began. Anglicanism has those things, and it has them in relatively neutral and accessible circumstances.

Anglicanism has the holy buildings, the prayer books, the daily offices, the *via media* that, from the beginning, asserted tradition and reason as well as Scripture as the bases of authority. And almost equally important – many would say even more important – it has, day after day, week after week, season after season, parament after parament and Scripture after Scripture, that glory-filled cycling of the liturgical year that ties all the parts of the Story together by reliving them year after year, until the whole pulses in one's consciousness like the ticking of an ancient clock.

Anglicanism has many other, less dramatic treasures, of course, ones that Emergence Christians would and will like to borrow, use and ultimately modify to their other and different contexts. Fresh expressions will do the same, though one would assume with greater breadth and perhaps more conservatively. But neither group will be Anglicans in the traditional or usual sense of that word, nor will they use the traditions received to pursue the Kingdom of God in the usual and customary ways.

Even anglimergents and/or fresh expressions, who by definition will be the Emergence Christians who stay nearest to home as we define it, will want to live where they worship and worship where they live on a routine basis; and that place of living and worshipping will not, in all probability, be elegant, much less middle-class acceptable. It will be, as was that of the early Church, among the hoi polloi, among those who often live out their years in less than privileged ways. And wherever the place of their worshipping is, it will above all else be a place that does not require guarding or monitoring. It will not be a place where the homeless are unwelcome, where the dirty are feared and the odoriferous scorned, where the hungry are suspect and the deranged shunned. Of that one thing, we may all be assured. But the place just might be ... ah, to think of such a thing! ... an Anglican church that is no longer home to a parish family or active congregation but that a diocese might see fit to convert to other uses for the kingdom rather than simply allow it to stand idle, unused and depreciating; or an Anglican building that presently is used at less than its full potential, but could be were it given to its fresh expressions and Emergence neighbours; or an Anglican parish where Taizé-like or Celtic or even traditional evensong are tailored consciously towards the needs of non-members who are that parish's anglimergence near-neighbours and so on.

In all of these and other possibilities, it is important, however, to understand one thing before the fact. That is, fresh expressions, as they live the Kingdom of God, will neither desire nor create the large parishes that were – and to a large extent still are – the *summa bonum* of Anglican history as well as of every church administrator with bills to pay. Nor will they see any need for a full-time priest. The homily is as easily and effectively given by a rotating list of fellow worshippers who study and pray and discern and who, therefore, can speak the word of God as purely and beneficially as can any of the ordained.

In similar fashion, the pastoral duties of prayer and visitation, support and counsel are patently the duties of the gathering community itself. Better a bivocational priest who worships with the community, consecrates the elements but does not necessarily administer them, and who can and willingly does support himself or herself financially. And better a missioner – for mission and missional are what any Emergence is – than a bishop, even if that same missioner is patently an interface or intermediary, as he or she must be, between the hierarchy and the fresh expression.

If these are the more obvious ways and means of fresh expressions in kingdom work and devotion, what then of the extant and larger church? Such, undoubtedly, is the subject of another extended essay, and even quite possibly of several volumes of extended essays. Better perhaps here to look instead at the insightful observations of another wise man who, like Robert Weber, is no longer with us physically, but remains alive in the work he left behind.

Ray Anderson taught for many years at Fuller Seminary. Like Weber, he was both a keen observer and credentialed theologian. In 2006, Anderson wrote, and InterVarsity Press published, a book entitled *An Emergent Theology for Emerging Churches*. While it is unusual for a book of contemporary observations to have a sustained shelf life, especially in roiling times like those of the Great Emergence, Anderson's has done just that, primarily, one must assume, because of its central argument.

In the beginning years of the faith, Anderson says, there was the church in Jerusalem and there was the church in Antioch. There was, that is, inherited Church and fresh expression of Church. It was by the mercy and grace of God, as well as by the grace and humility of Christians in Jerusalem and Christians in Antioch, that inherited Church felt concern for, as well as because of, what was happening in those distant fresh expressions. Accordingly, Jerusalem sent Paul and Barnabas to investigate, counsel, evaluate. But it also was through the mercy and grace of God and of the believers in both bodies that Antioch both received the ecclesial visitors and then themselves sent emissaries and messages of respect back to Jerusalem to discuss further matters of praxis and conduct.

The differences between inherited and fresh expressions were never entirely resolved. Tensions remained. And save for one small purse in a time of great need, Jerusalem never received any direct benefit from Antioch. What benefited, Anderson points out, was and is the kingdom. And, Anderson also says, given all of that, we now can do no less, regardless of which camp we may choose to worship and serve in. May it prove to be among us as he has said.

Note

1 The material in this paragraph of the present discussion first appeared in *patheos* in the issue of 9 August 2010 under the title of 'The Great Emergence [of] Christianity: Changing the World' and has been reprinted in various places subsequently.

7

Christian Family Centre: Mission, Discipleship and Transformation

PAUL PAYNTER

'Where the Spirit of the Lord is there is freedom' (2 Cor. 3.17). At Christian Family Centre, Northern Ireland (CFC), this is our founding principle, our daily inspiration and purpose, and our ongoing hope. We are only too aware that the issues faced here at CFC are most difficult, but we know that the resources of the Trinity are more than sufficient to meet and transform even the darkest of situations. We exist because we have and continue to experience the freedom of being in Christ, and our deepest desire is that others, especially those suffering the bondage of addiction, would also know for themselves this freeing Spirit – not just freedom in the area of their most obvious need, but freedom into everything that Jesus desires for them.[1] In sum, we seek to live as priests of the Kingdom of God, to build kingdom bridges that assist others to break the bonds that have held them captive and landed them in prison.

From depression to compassion: a story of liberation

Suella Strydom walked out of yet another counselling session frustrated and angry. As she walked along the street in Petermaritzburg, South Africa, she noticed three children sitting on the street corner, begging for a little food or money. 'Why can't I get myself sorted and help little ones like these?' was the thought that came from somewhere deep inside her. For years Suella had been addicted to various drugs, but no matter what type of treatment or therapy she tried, the change was only temporary.

At the age of 11 Suella committed her life to Jesus Christ and did follow him for a few years. At 16 she started smoking dope and from then on substance abuse became part of her life, and all the wrong relationships that go with that. In 2003 Suella left South Africa to be with her family in England, and she promised herself that she would never return to South Africa with all its unhappy memories. However, Suella's life in England continued as before, degenerating into an uncontrollable mess.

In May 2005 Suella stopped using all illegal drugs, but quickly fell into deep depression. She was constantly anxious, and condemning thoughts about her past controlled her mind. Making any good choices about her future seemed almost impossible. Yet again, Suella's family stepped in to help, and she went to live with her mum. However, she continued to withdraw into herself, avoided communication with anyone and hardly ever left her bed – never mind her room. Hospitalization now seemed the only route open to her.

Suella then heard about the ministry of CFC in Northern Ireland. She made contact with my wife, Kerry, and I, and we invited her for an assessment. She had no idea what to expect, and the fear of rejection almost put her off even trying. Suella was accepted at CFC and moved here in January 2006. At first she didn't like being at the Centre at all, but felt deep within herself that this was her last chance. Living with others was a real challenge and many times she felt like giving up. Also, for the first time in 13 years Suella was not altering her mood with any substances and now had to face her own thoughts and feelings without an 'easy' way of escape.

One of the first lessons Suella learned at CFC was that she must stop comparing herself to those around her, and humbly receive God's mercy and grace for herself. She was learning to renew her own thinking and bring it into line with the truth of God's word. She was learning that who we are in Christ is more important than any other identity. Slowly but surely she began to change and started to experience God restoring her. One of the main changes in Suella was the way that she viewed God: instead of seeing God as a harsh taskmaster she started to see God as a good father. This revelation of God as her Father was a springboard into real healing and lasting change.

After 11 months of changes and challenges Suella now contemplated her future in a different light. The dream of helping others, especially children, was coming alive again. Suella was encouraged to do 'normal life' for a period of time and then see what God opened up for her. A family connected with CFC offered Suella a place in their home and she got a job in a recruitment agency. Some months later she had got her own place again, and was becoming more and more integrated into the life of a local church fellowship. Suella's journey towards freedom was continuing.

The desire to help abandoned children was getting stronger and stronger but Suella wasn't sure what the next step was. In December 2006 she went to visit a children's home in Vryheid, South Africa. There she discovered that the leaders of Inkulueko Children's Home had heard about her, through her sister, many years before and prayed that God would save her from drugs. God started to speak to Suella about returning to South Africa, the country she had promised herself she would never return to.

In May 2007 Suella Strydom left Northern Ireland for Vryheid to work full-time at Inkulueko Children's Home. The dream that was birthed in her heart when she was living a life of pain and rebellion far away from God is now becoming a reality. Interestingly, in Suella's native language Vryheid means 'freedom'.

A little history

CFC is located in the County Antrim village of Armoy, Northern Ireland. It exists to provide pastoral care to anyone who is hurting, especially those who have been affected by addictions of any kind. Since CFC opened in 1990, people have sought help here from all over the UK and Ireland, and other places around the world such as Holland and South Africa. Some have come for one-off prayer ministry and counsel; others have come to stay for many months, in order to work through some of the most complex issues that human beings can face.

CFC has its genesis in the transformed lives of David and Linda Hoy. Alcohol abuse, on David's part, had almost physically destroyed him, and had had a negative impact on his marriage and family. However, in the late 1980s, as the Hoys responded to the good news of Jesus Christ and his kingdom, their lives took on a radical new direction. Almost immediately after their conversion they began to understand that God was commissioning them to help others who found themselves in circumstances similar to their own. They sensed that God wanted them to pioneer a ministry that would provide refuge to people trapped by all kinds of trouble, but especially those overwhelmed by addiction. So without any capital or visible means of support, they left their business and home community to pursue the call that they believed God was putting on their lives. David and Linda's own transformation provides the foundational hope for our ministry to individuals and families that are affected by addiction. This good news, the Hoys and we at CFC believe, can and does transform lives, families, and even whole communities.

Loving into freedom

By the time our guests arrive with us their lives have usually become pretty chaotic, so there is an immediate need for a disciplined routine. Time is allotted for Bible study – as part of a group and individually – and for personal pastoral mentoring. There is also a focus on practical work, and so we have fully equipped wood and metal workshops, as well as a polytunnel for growing plants and vegetables. We seek to provide practical work not as time-filler but primarily as an aid to the therapeutic process. We are physical, bodied beings and our journey of healing will reflect this. Times of silence and solitude, and just plain 'free time', are also factored into the weekly routine, so that there is time to think and reflect. We have discovered that silence and solitude is advantageous for spiritual formation generally, but for those who formerly abused substances, it is almost essential for dealing appropriately with real thoughts and feelings. They need to learn how to do 'bored' if they are ever going to live without sensual stimulation (the same goes for non-substance abusers as well).

At the beginning of someone's stay at CFC the boundaries around them are pretty fixed, so that almost every outside influence is controlled. But this is only a temporary phase and the goal is to move as quickly as possible towards self-enforced protective boundaries. We try to encourage change from the inside out and not the other way around. An institutionalized environment of rules and regulations won't do that.

At the Centre we encourage and train our guests to bring their whole lives under the rule of God in order for them to be transformed. We want them to see that making Jesus the Lord of their past, present and future is the best way to live. If you are ever given permission to truly hear the history of someone who is addicted to or is abusing substances, you will likely discover a background story that has led to their using (and choosing) substance abuse as a way of numbing pain. There are often various kinds of trauma that have deeply impacted and defined their internal view of how life really is.

It is our claim that the good news, which is manifested supremely in Jesus, is that we don't have to deal with life independent of God any longer; we don't have to cope with the consequences of life's experiences and traumas on our own. The good news is that we can rethink the orientation of our lives because the Kingdom of God has come near, is within our grasp. We believe that what the scriptural model of discipleship reveals about God, humanity and the world around us should be the dominant paradigm for dealing with those who are addicted to or abusing substances. Therefore, we describe the relationship between a person's negative history and their current wrong choices by saying that 'there may an explanation for the choices you are making, but there is no excuse for the choices that you are making'. There is another way to deal with life. This liberates people to take responsibility for their own choices while at the same time enabling them to find release and healing from their past. However, working all these implications through takes time, sometimes quite a lot of time; that's why we don't put a limit on the length of our guests' stay. Most are with us for quite a number of months, but even when they're leaving we don't claim that their transformation is complete. In truth, we will all walk somewhat wounded until God's Kingdom comes and his will is done on earth as it is in the heavens. We have to keep that not-yet-whole reality in mind, while pushing into the present kingdom reality for the greater wholeness Jesus promised us here and now.

'Tell me, how can I be free?'

We are all looking for the magic formula, the quick fix; a tried and tested method that produces predictable solutions, fast. At CFC we have no such fixed programme, but a way of life, a way of living that is informed by the inbreaking Kingdom of God. We seek to live in the light of this new reality, choosing not to remain bound by the deceit of the world, the flesh and the devil, as the Book of Common Prayer puts it. At CFC the overt goal is that people will deal with the causes and consequences of their addiction or substance abuse by becoming disciples of Jesus Christ. We are disciples of Christ, and our hope is that as we and our guests journey through life together for a stage they will encounter Jesus in us and know him personally. We want them to see Jesus, to bump into his goodness, to run into his love, to glimpse his abundance, his mercy, his grace, his delight in them, as we simply share everyday life together.

People who come to stay with us do not have to be Christians, however the reality is that the majority have some kind of connection with Christians or Church. Indeed, this is how most find out about us, because we don't advertise for clients. We have found that most people need a fresh (or perhaps more accurately, a Godly) narrative of God – even though they may not be aware of it! Others don't know exactly what they need or what they are looking for, but what they do acknowledge is that they need help. Generally speaking, by the time they arrive with us, our guests are in a poor state financially, phys-ically, emotionally and spiritually. What they need is a safe place to regain or discover their true dignity as human persons made in the image of God – a gentle God, who does not break the bruised reed or quench the dimly burning wick; a just and faithful God who relentlessly fights for wholeness.

How then can I be free? We invite people to come and expe-rience God's presence, believing that freedom reigns in this place, and is available to all who allow Jesus to reign in their lives, just as they are, knowing that God loves them too dearly to leave them just as they are.

Discipleship: a non-negotiable

It is our contention at CFC that there is a need for those who self-identify as evangelical Christians to rethink the meaning of 'disciple', and what we mean when we speak of 'disciple-ship'. Do we think that discipleship is an optional bolt-on to a conversion experience that prepares us for life after death but not before? Do we actually believe that discipleship is essential in order to be Christian? Dallas Willard argues that there is a primacy placed on discipleship in the New Testament texts (1999, p. 258). He writes,

> The word disciple occurs 269 times in the New Testament. 'Christian' is found three times and was first introduced to refer precisely to the disciples – in a situation where it was no longer possible to regard them as a sect of the Jews (Acts 11.26). The New Testament is a book about disciples, by disciples, and for disciples of Jesus Christ.

Actually learning to think and act like Jesus himself was the default position of those who were first identified as Christians. Therefore a Christian is, by definition, a Christ-follower, a dis-ciple, a person choosing a lifetime of discipleship with, for and in, Christ. This is an important point for us at CFC and we define what we do as discipleship rather than just recovery or rehabilitation. Of course, true discipleship is not exclusive of recovery or rehabilitation. We do not class CFC as a rehabilitation centre for addicts, but rather a place where people can be taught to search out what discipleship, or apprenticeship to Jesus might look like for their own life, no matter how messed up and out of control their life has been, and perhaps still is.

Jesus taught that those who would become his disciples would be liberated from the controlling power of sin, from the oppressive, fearful and guilt-ridden consequences of their unwise decisions and abuse suffered. He promised that they would know the truth and that this truth would set them free (John 8.31–32). So our intention is to create a safe environment that is conducive to discipleship, where people can step out of their 'normal' environment for a while and take time to (re)connect purposefully with God, and with themselves, thus freeing them from the things that are holding their lives in bondage. We provide a place where people can live, work and study together in a way that assists discipleship to Jesus Christ. The way we do this in practice has been evolving as we discover fresh truths that are beneficial in helping people work out what discipleship looks like for them. Again, we are not trying to impose a method, but introduce them to a relationship – *the* relationship – that will, in turn, transform everything else.

Milestones on the road to freedom

One of the highlights of what happens at Christian Family Centre is water baptisms (which usually take place in the Irish Sea, even in winter!). We view these events as the happiest funerals that we get to go to. It is amazing to witness people turn their back on their past and identify with Jesus in his death, burial and resurrection. People we have baptized have often said later on that their baptism was the defining moment or the turning point of their time spent with us. It is not that they never had any issues to deal with after that, but they find that things are never quite the same after being baptized. People who connect with the potential of a new identity and a new life 'in Christ' discover their view of themselves changes. What we endeavour to do is to help people live out this new identity of being in Christ for their own unique life. Everything we do is geared towards helping people live out the paradox of being in Christ, which is like already being somewhere and still needing to make the journey to get there.

One of the most frequent questions that we are asked about the centre is 'What is the success rate?'

While generally knowing what people mean when they ask that sort of question, our response is to ask questions in reply. What does 'success' look like for the people that we are trying to help? Does it mean that they stay sober? Does it mean that they don't use drugs anymore? For us that is not success. Our goal is to see transformation of a life from the inside out, so how would it be possible to measure such change in any meaningful and scientific way? How do you measure the results of discipleship? Therefore we choose not to try to do so. Obviously, for someone who has been really struggling with drug or alcohol abuse, external change may be observed and appreciated quite easily.

It has been our privilege to watch many people who were merely struggling to survive, find real purpose and significance beyond just existing and actually living life. Whenever I am asked the 'statistic question' I am not inclined to think of numbers but instead I bring the names and faces of people to my mind. Many faces come to mind, some of whom did very well after leaving the Centre but then returned to former habits. Some do well most of the time but go in cycles and never totally stay clean. It is also true that others have died without any visible transformation taking place. This is the hard reality of ministering to those who are addicted. We are in a battle; battling for the lives of those Satan seeks to destroy. It is not a battle of equals though. Where the Spirit of the Lord is, *there is freedom*. However, freedom must be chosen every day; Christ will not force it upon us. Sometimes we wish he would!

Conclusion

It is our privilege at CFC to witness lives once bound by addiction freed by Christ. It is heartbreaking to watch some choose to continue in their deathly ways without Christ. The answer, as any child in Sunday school will tell you, is Jesus. The simplicity of this truth can embarrass, irritate or even offend some, but we have learned to embrace such child-like theology. As uninhibited children of God we want to shout from the rooftops about the good news of the kingdom, the good news of Jesus Christ that liberates, that transforms those affected by addiction. Jesus invites you, not to a programme, but into the relationship of a lifetime. This is what we want to communicate in everything we do at CFC; to embody and facilitate discipleship to Jesus that transforms every day, every decision and every relationship. We are not about techniques, coping strategies, offering support in a 'meet once a week, study a manual' kind of way. We want to assist people to deal with the root issues in their lives and not just get them 'sober', so that they may be free from addiction, and freed for abundant life in Christ.

Choose freedom.

Note

1 Isaiah 61.1: 'The Spirit of the Lord God is upon me, because the Lord has anointed me; he has sent me to bring good news to the oppressed, to bind up the broken-hearted, to proclaim liberty to the captives, and release to the prisoners.'

8

Kingdom and Crystals

DIANA GREENFIELD

Walking down the High Street as Glastonbury wakes up, I am bombarded with the psychedelic colours, smells and sounds that accost my senses. The first person to speak to me is Gina, a local photographer whom I haven't seen for a while, who always wears odd shoes. She comments on the feather and sparkles in my hair, describing me as the funkiest vicar she has ever known. From across the road comes Tony, who always calls me 'lady' and describes himself as 'knight and scholar'. He's someone who chooses to seek my point of view on how to handle the difficulties life throws at him, but I have had to earn his trust, and often I think it is still a fragile gift. These are the ordinary and yet extraordinary people of Glastonbury, those who wrestle with what it is to live in a liminal place where the spiritual and the earthly world are extremely close together.

Through the arch into Glastonbury Abbey and I enter a different world, one of the ancient ruins scattered around, reminding visitors of an era long gone when the Church ruled the world. It is a tranquil place in the heart of the town, and yet forgotten. Many of the locals only ever visit for rock concerts and fireworks, an iconic backdrop for an extravaganza of sound. Today it is quiet in St Patrick's Chapel with its candle light and musty smelling vestments. Seven other people join me to celebrate Holy Communion. I think the words of *Common Worship* seem too many, and maybe even too modern for this place. This is a site where Christians have worshipped for almost 2,000 years, where pioneers have brought the gospel in a new way, over and over, and where I am doing the same.

In April 2010 I took up the post of Avalon Pioneer Minister. Geographically, Avalon is the local ministry group area of Street, Walton, Glastonbury and Meare. The primary aim of the role as written in the job description is:

The main focus of the post will involve reaching out to the ordinary people of the towns and villages who do not, or have not attended church. One of the facets of this appointment would be to find new ways in which the Church can be relevant for them, either in their own local communities or through the existing churches. In essence, the post would be evangelistic/outreach but the person would have to have a desire to serve these communities in being 'church' wherever the people are – both geographically, culturally and spiritually.

There is a twisting and twining of the spiritual influences in this town that goes back to within 60 years of Christ's death and resurrection. It would be impossible to untangle the myth from the legend, from the Christian or the pagan, but somehow the gospel message still belongs. I think it is my job, through relationships and encounters, to bring that same message the early Christians brought, but in a way that touches the lives of those living in Glastonbury today.

This small area is incredibly diverse. Street is the home of Clarks Village, a shopping outlet that attracts over one million visitors a year. Walton and Mere are both rural villages with their own identities, and then there is Glastonbury. For this chapter, I'm going to focus on Glastonbury, as the town represents the greatest diversity of spiritual seekers imaginable.

In any pioneer role it is important to start out by getting to know a community, to understand it, to discover what its influences are spiritually, geographically, culturally. To use Walter Winks' terminology, in *Unmasking the Powers*, it is about identifying the angel who represents the characteristics of the community. In Glastonbury this is a difficult task. There are so many layers and an incredible amount of history – it was hard to know where to start.

One of the most helpful things that happened when I first arrived was the showing of a film called *Glastonbury: The Untold Story* by a historian of myth and religion, Dr Tim Hopkinson Ball. It gave me an insight into what makes the town tick and introduced me to some of the historical and spiritual themes that have been key to the identity the town.

There is a wealth of Christian heritage in Glastonbury. It is believed that Joseph of Arimathea came to the town 2,000 years ago, and there are some who like to believe he may have brought his young nephew Jesus. What is certain is that an Abbey was founded in the seventh century, which by the fourteenth century was the second wealthiest in the country after Westminster Abbey. The town is still dominated by the abbey ruins, one of the main tourist attractions alongside the Tor. There is also a pre-Christian heritage to the town as it is thought to be the Celtic isle of Avalon, the isle of enchantment. Celtic legend believed that the Tor was hollow and an entrance to the Celtic underworld.

Another legendary figure associated with the town is King Arthur. Some think Glastonbury was Arthur's Camelot. The Tor has been a feature of goddess worship found in both Celtic and Arthurian legends. Glastonbury has been considered a sacred place for many thousands of years, but the spiritual mix that is available in the town has intensified over the last forty years.

Many of the older people who live in Glastonbury remember it as a perfectly ordinary market town, with 'normal' shops in the high street. The main industry was sheepskin manufacture and the two main employers in the town were Moorlands and Baileys.

Forty years ago a farmer in Pilton (six miles up the road) held a music festival for about 1,500 people. The following year the festival was moved to a date coinciding with the summer solstice. The Glastonbury Festival at Worthy Farm now attracts over 100,000 for the festival weekend. The 2011 festival was like an A–Z of music dignitaries, with U2 to Beyoncé to Coldplay performing.

Interestingly, even the festival has taken on some of Glastonbury's ancient identity. The now iconic Pyramid Stage was built on the ley line between Glastonbury and Stonehenge, thus enforcing the link between Glastonbury and spiritual seekers, initially known as New Agers. Some of those seekers stayed on in the town after the festival, making it their home. Now they form a healthy proportion of the permanent population of Glastonbury, having settled down and raised families in the town.

Over the last forty years the town has gone through a major transformation, and is now known as a mecca for spiritual seekers from far and wide. Many of the shops now cater for the spiritual tourists, who are often seeking healing crystals, some form of spiritual experience, or clothes to make them look the part. They say of Glastonbury that if you can't find the religion you are looking for then they'll invent one for you. If you have never visited then you are missing a treat: it is a spiritual pick 'n' mix like nothing you will experience anywhere else.

What I soon recognized is that much of what is available to buy on the high street are cheap, spiritual tourist trinkets – just as you might expect to buy a stick of rock in Blackpool, you buy a crystal with healing properties in Glastonbury. However, if one looks beyond the tourism, there are many spiritual seekers.

So how have I started out in mission to spiritual seekers? As I reflect on this question in relation to my first eighteen months of ministry in Glastonbury, I realize that I really haven't done too much. I don't mean that I have done nothing, in fact I have been very busy, but what has kept me busy are the encounters that God has brought about. As I have prayed I have met the most amazing people and encountered incredible possibilities where the Christians can, or are already, engaging in the wider community. I did wonder whether the best offer for this chapter would be ten blank pages with the heading 'PRAY AND GOD WILL DO IT!' Interestingly the one thing that I wanted to be involved with, for selfish reasons, has not come about due to a series of complications, and I have taken a step away from it.

Often in the past people have asked me why I do what I do. The flippant answer I have always given is: because of God. I don't mean that a deeper answer wouldn't involve God, but that if it wasn't what God wanted I wouldn't do it. I am by nature passionate, enthusiastic and pragmatic, and I want more than anything to see things happen. But I have learned that things only happen if they are the will of God.

Romans 12.2 says 'Do not conform any longer to the pattern of this world, but be transformed by the renewing of your mind. Then you will be able to test and approve what God's will is – his good, pleasing and perfect will.'

I often describe this sense in relationship to sanding a piece of wood. If you sand with the grain it feels right even if it is at times quite hard, but if you sand against the grain it feels wrong and scratches the wood. For me the same is true of pioneer ministry. Sometimes the sanding process might take a long while and the same is true of mission, but with patience and trust in God we can learn to go with his will, rather than against it.

One of the things that I noticed almost as soon as I arrived was that despite the numerous spiritual seekers the mainstream Christian churches are struggling to make their voices heard. Most of the church congregations are elderly and while there are pockets of enthusiasm for the gospel it seems that Christianity has been sidelined in favour of more colourful or experiential spiritualities. I was very uncomfortable to discover that members of the churches referred to the spiritual seekers in the town as 'alternatives', as it seemed such a dismissive term. However, I soon learned that the title is one the spiritual seekers have owned for themselves, and at times they band together as the 'alternatives' in the town. Anyone who has chosen to follow a spiritual path that is not Christianity tends to consider themself alternative. The other factor that seems to unite the alternatives is a great sense of commitment to environment issues.

The question becomes where on earth does one begin in this context to present the Kingdom of God in a relevant way? Archbishop Rowan has often been quoted as saying that mission is to see what God is doing and join in. With this in mind I have spent the first six months in my new role trying to work this out. I have been challenged and excited by the opportunities that have come about, and I am consistently being surprised.

The one thing that I knew when I began was that to be truly culturally missional I needed to leave behind all personal agendas and learn about the town, meet some of the key players and discern where God was already working.

One of the verses that echoes in my mind in relation to Glastonbury is 1 Corinthians 9.22b: 'I have become all things to all people, that by all means I might save some.'

Spiritual seekers are not looking for people to give them an absolute truth, they are looking for people to seek with them, to travel some of their spiritual journey with them. I am more than willing to be a spiritual seeker with them and hopefully in doing so I will learn more about my own faith. It would be naive not to recognize that there are risks involved in being willing to engage with other spiritualities, but as Christians we believe that God is creator of all things and is in all things. My own personal line in the sand is that while I will journey and observe other styles of worship, my own worship will be for God alone.

There is a small complex in the town comprising a simple, atmospheric chapel dedicated to St Margaret of Scotland, a peaceful garden area and three historic almshouses. It is a space that attracts people for its peace, simplicity and inclusivity. Recently a new charity has been formed to care for the site, organize renovations and make the complex more available to those who appreciate it. I have spent a couple of afternoons simply sitting in the garden and have been totally surprised by the number of people who have come through the doors just because they were open, many of whom would not set foot in a more conventional church building.

One group who regularly uses the building is a collection of people who enjoy singing Taizé. Through a slightly complicated series of events I have found myself leading the group. In doing so, I arranged to spend the evening with the lady who originally started the group. When I checked with a friend who knew her, I was advised that the one subject to avoid was Christianity. As it turned out, much of the conversation revolved around Christianity and community; suffice it to say, she was the one who introduced the subject. She would most definitely be considered an 'alternative' and was a bit suspicious that any community involvement the Church might have would turn out to be just a recruitment drive; and yet she was far from antagonistic. We both had a really enjoyable evening and are planning to do another; and she has agreed to come back and share responsibility for the Taizé group she started. This is just one example of the many conversations I have had with people around the town. The preconception is often that the Church wants to recruit people. The challenge becomes to introduce people to the Kingdom of God without their thinking it is a conscription exercise. I think the only way to do that is to build honest relationship with people without an agenda to convert.

The Taizé singing group is made up of people from all backgrounds and spiritualities, who want to express how they feel through their voices. With integrity I would like to think the singing group will be nothing more than that, but with the intentionality of mission I hope that it will be an access point for people wanting to encounter God.

On another occasion, again in St Margaret's Chapel, we had an open day, during which I introduced some of the activities that the Dekhomai stand offers at Mind Body Spirit festivals. We offered prayer beads, foot massaging, and Jesus Deck readings. I spent much of the day massaging people's feet and hearing of their spiritual journeys. The wonderful difference in doing this in Glastonbury rather than at an MBS festival is that many of the people I met were town people whom I have seen again since, so rather than simply being a one-off act of kindness, it becomes the start of a shared journey, and only God knows where that will take us.

Not long after I arrived, the person responsible for a late-night coffee project in Frome contacted me. I also met the local policeman, who told me that they were very keen for something like this to start in Glastonbury. Slowly I have been sowing the idea around the churches in the town as something we can do as Christians to serve the community. Slowly it is starting to gather momentum. Quite unexpectedly a lady approached me and offered to pay for a van. I also followed up a meeting with someone I had been told would be interesting for me to meet, only to discover he was chairman of the local PACT committee; he was incredibly enthusiastic about the idea and wanted it to happen straight away. There are many people in Glastonbury who need to encounter the Kingdom of God, not just those who would consider themselves spiritual seekers. A late-night coffee van in Glastonbury run by Christians is a powerful witness to the values of the Kingdom of God that is outside of institutional Church. While in some ways this project may not be aimed at serving spiritual seekers, I am certain that it is God's will, and so, although it feels right to be patient, it is an initiative that I am investing my energies in.

I have not been surprised that the spiritual seekers I have spent time with are closed to the institutional Church, but what has constantly surprised me is their openness to the ways of the Kingdom of God, and often how much they actually know about Christianity. Over the years there have been attempts to start alternative Christian communities in Glastonbury that tap into this, although for one reason or another they have not survived. I do believe that God's will is to see a community of spiritual seekers who can encounter his kingdom in a way that is appropriate to them, but as yet I am not sure how that will happen. I can only continue to do what I have started by praying that his kingdom will come, and see what happens.

The real voyage of discovery consists not in seeking new landscapes, but in having new eyes. (Marcel Proust)

Reference

Walter Wink, 1986, *Unmasking the Powers*, Minneapolis: Augsburg Fortress.

9

How Serious is it Really?
The Mixed Economy and the
Light-hearted Long Haul

LINCOLN HARVEY

Introductory comments

The question of fresh expressions is partly to do with the shape of the Church. What is the right form for a discerning Church to take in these particular times and in this particular place? Of course, this question is not a new question. It's been around since the Church began. Yet some new answers to it are beginning to emerge within Western culture. Christians are searching for imaginative ways to be a gospel-shaped community, alive to – and within – the missional realities of contemporary life. An experiment is clearly underway, and its outcome is largely unknown.

With these experimental patterns of life overlapping and intertwining inherited forms of Church, a mixed – and somewhat muddled – economy exists.[1] Like any economy, the mixed economy is characterized by a complex web of interrelationship and exchange. Helpful ideas and practices are traded across different times and traditions, with pioneering practitioners drawing lessons from both past and present as they seek to discern the shape of the Church's future within their own locality. And in similar fashion, new ideas for mission are being folded back into inherited models of Church, thereby establishing new and dynamic enterprises within the context of the local parish. The mixed economy appears in good health.

However, a less charitable currency also circulates within the economy. I myself discovered this a few years back, when commissioned to design a distinct pathway for pioneer ministers through a traditional training programme. Keen to discover the best design for the pathway, I entered into consultation with a number of people engaged with the emerging churches. This process involved some fascinating conversations, many of which included inspirational stories about contemporary Christians living out the gospel imaginatively amid the unchurched today. But through the course of these testimonies I began to sense how many pioneers consider the parish system to be dead on its feet. The unspoken message seemed clear: fresh expressions are the future, the parish history, and time will tell.

During this period of consultation, I continued to work with candidates placed on more traditional routes towards public ministry, as well as myself ministering in inherited forms of Church. In these contexts, I was again privileged to hear Christians speak of their desire to share the gospel, this time as missioners to the unchurched from within more traditional settings. I was often quizzed on my research, with people keen to know what I thought of the emerging churches. In these conversations, it was the validity of fresh expressions that was now being questioned, with novel forms of Church regularly dismissed as a flash in the pan. The message was again clear: fresh expressions have no future, they are a sell-out to culture, and – again – time will tell.

Leaving aside the merits of charge and counter-charge, it became obvious that fresh expressions divide opinion. Christians tend to see them either as a living hope for the future *or* instead an irritating distraction from the serious business of established life. In both instances, the mixed economy is reduced to a passing phenomenon. People tend to believe that innovation *or* stability will emerge victorious, with the mixed economy read as some sort of evolutionary struggle in the species called Church. With the threat of extinction hanging in the air, people understandably get defensive, being quick to highlight weaknesses in other forms of Church in the hope that

their favoured way proves the enduring way. In this environment, anxious opinion becomes polarized as the competitive
subplot casts its shadow across the economy.

The competitive subplot to the mixed economy also means
the debate about fresh expressions is in some sense *inflationary*.
The pressurized market – and fears about competitive rivals –
encourage Christians of all shapes and sizes to overvalue the
importance of their own form of Church. It's easy to think that
what we're doing is more valuable or more worthy than what
others are doing. Again – anecdotally – the debate about the
emerging churches is very serious in character. People are *seriously* into antinominalism, antitraditionalism, anticlericalism
and so on. The question, however, is whether things would be
this way if we believed the mixed economy were here to stay.
Would we become a bit less defensive – the question of fresh
expressions a bit less serious – if we were able to accept that the
mixed economy was not a passing phenomenon? And could
we then let go of our self-importance if we accepted long-term
communion with those who hear the call of God differently?

It is with questions such as these in mind that this chapter is
written. I remain, in many respects, an outsider to the debate
about fresh expressions, especially since completing my work
in curriculum design. Yet – despite feeling a sense of detached
observation! – I remain convinced that the debate is somewhat
overheated and marked too often by self-importance. As a
result, I want to throw a couple of ideas into the mix to tem-
per discussions. The ideas may not appear directly relevant,
and might take readers some distance from their concerns
about church order and mission. Nevertheless, I think the ideas
should be helpful because they qualify discussions by placing
them within a broad theological framework. That is to say, the
story of the mixed economy is part of the older story of God
with his creatures.

To this end, the aim of the chapter is somewhat ambitious –
and might be the equivalent of using a sledgehammer to crack
a nut! I first want to tackle the way in which we overvalue one
side of the mixed economy – whatever 'side' that might be – at
the expense of the other. This section of the chapter is under-

written by the belief that Jesus is teaching us to cultivate 'a weak-sense of self-importance', as Ellen Charry puts it (1997, p. 78). This part of the argument will draw on what we know about the nature of creation in light of the Church's traditional teaching, especially the way in which the created order – of which fresh expressions remain a part! – is to be understood as intrinsically *non-serious*. By bringing the irreducibly non-serious nature of existence to the fore, I hope to show that the mixed economy should be light-hearted in character.[2] (Or to put it otherwise, church order is never worth killing for!) Having made this somewhat obvious point, I will proceed to draw out one feature of the argument to identify a reason why we might expect the mixed – and somewhat muddled – economy to endure. Here the argument will turn from creation to God, allowing the Church's traditional teaching on the Trinity to inform our perspective on the mixed economy. This part of the chapter will depend on a working assumption that God's own economy – his handiwork, so to speak – 'reflects' his eternal nature. If this assumption is allowed, it enables us to reimagine the mixed economy and see it as a lively reality, appropriately reflecting the dynamic and loving interrelation that is God the Father, Son and Holy Spirit. With this recognized, it could allow us to enjoy the apparent tensions in the mixed economy, thereby celebrating the positive interplay of innovation and stability, continuity and change that the current situation demonstrates. In effect, given *God*, the mixed economy is hopefully a sustainable economy, so prepare for the light-hearted long haul!

As these introductory comments suggest, the chapter will involve some *theology*. Theology often gets a bad press amid pioneers. It's sometimes understood as an imperial exercise in thought-control, restricting free exploration and a means by which the established Church imposes relative ideas under the guise of absolute truths. Such criticism is mistaken on many levels, but here – to alleviate any possible fears – we need only distinguish between the practice and product of theology. As a practice, theology is simply the non-offensive skill of allowing our faithful understandings of God, creation and Jesus Christ to mutually inform and shape one another in order to make meaningful sense of God and the world and our place in both.[3] As a piece of theology, therefore, the argument of this chapter seeks to understand our place in the contemporary mixed economy by linking the discussion to an understanding of what it means to be a creature created by a dynamic and lively God. It is to place our testimonies within the story that gives them primary sense.

Nevertheless, this is not an attempt to end the debate about church order; nor am I suggesting that the question is in any sense trivial. Church is a serious business (and mission is a serious business), as history clearly demonstrates.[4] It will no doubt remain important to ask questions about ecclesial and missional identities – with an understanding of the authoritative role of Scripture, creeds, and sacramental life surely central to Christian answers to them.[5] Yet within the space available – within the varied dialectics and accents of the language *Christianese*, as it might be put (Jenson, 1997, p. 18) – we should not take what we believe about the shape of the Church too seriously, nor assume that the mixed economy is some sort of temporary phenomenon. If we are clear on these points, then the ongoing conversation might become more charitable *and* more outwardly focused as our anxious self-importance is reduced and our differences are celebrated.

1 The non-serious character of the creature[6]

Christians traditionally believe that God created the world 'out of nothing'.[7] This difficult – but important – doctrine establishes a number of theological points. First, 'nothing' is not some kind of a 'thing' from which God struggled to shape the world. Instead, it denotes *nothing*, and so it makes the claim that God miraculously summoned the creature into life. Or otherwise put, there is only *one* God. Second, 'nothing' is not some kind of *need* in God. We would be wrong to envisage 'nothing' as some kind of divine deficiency, a 'gap' that so to speak, God needed to fill in order to be satisfied. Instead, Christians understand God to be perfect and complete in himself. The 'completeness' of God makes it a mistake to imagine God all alone in eternity (maybe bored and lonely!) and therefore *needing* to create in order to have something to love.[8] The Church does not believe God needed something to love because we believe that God keeps his own company, so to speak. He *is* the eternal communion of three persons-in-relation, Father, Son and Holy Spirit. Consequently, when the triune God – who *is* loving communion – chose to create the world, he did not do so from some intrinsic need. Instead, he did it *gracefully*. And this means that creation signifies freedom; it was not necessary. God freely summoned us out of nothing. This is the key point.

The non-necessary character of creation allows us to see that we are not that 'serious', as Rowan Williams puts it. For Williams, the doctrine of creation means that we are 'poised on the divine word, the divine communication over an unfathomable abyss'. Because we are not necessary, we are – as the products of free creation – essentially groundless, without support, with no 'density and solidity' other than that which we receive as a gift from God. But as Williams makes clear, this dizzying groundlessness to our life is not to be confused with some kind of meaningless nihilism. In fact it is the opposite. He writes:

[O]ut of all this comes the miracle ... the recognition that my reality rests 'like a feather on the breath of God'. It *is* because God speaks, because God loves and it *is* for no other reason. And if we want to know what it *is* to say that I *am*, the only answer is 'I *am* because of the love of God'. And when I seek to justify, defend or systematize what I am, I become 'serious'. I cease to be a feather on the breath of God and gravity draws me down into darkness.[9]

As Williams understands it, we *are* the not-serious-yet-freely-loved creatures. This non-serious freedom is not a chaotic freedom, however, where anything goes in some sort of arbitrary force of will, some brute capricious plurality. Instead, we exist for a reason: God created in order to share his life generously with a 'fourth'. Creation is therefore to be understood as the bringing into existence of that which is not God by a free sovereign act of *love* for the purpose of gracious communion. Love is the meaning of our unnecessary existence.

As we can see here, the Christian doctrine of creation implies that we are fundamentally non-serious, yet meaningfully loved. The very fabric of our lives – the *creatureliness* of our existence, we might say – *is* delightful, the end of graceful love, which suggests that our attempts to defend or justify what we are somehow miss the truth of our existence. This is perhaps why a saint such as Francis of Assisi remains so influential within the Church.[10] His wandering life of radical simplicity – his tireless work to rebuild Christ's Church – was underwritten by his sense of being a fool for God. Francis *played* because he accepted that he was a *creature* set amid contingent creatures, all of whom he embraced in charity, and all for whom he endlessly gave thanks.[11] And so it was the non-serious shape to his life that allowed Francis to celebrate the Church both in its reforming novelty and traditional stability, as he shared with everyone the love of God revealed in his Lord and saviour. For Francis, therefore, a muddled economy of settled and itinerant Christians, amid novel spontaneity within the order of the established Church, was not a problem to be solved because he refused to confuse himself with anything *that* important. In effect, St Francis knew his doctrine of creation and was therefore able to embrace the traditional and the novel. We would do well to do the same. Whatever we're doing, we're not that serious. Seriousness might be the tragic sin that undermines a gospel-shaped creation.

2 The mixed economy of God

Alongside the doctrine of creation, Christians believe that God is Father, Son and Holy Spirit. By confessing the Trinity, we say what we have to say about Israel's God *given* the endless event of Christ and the Spirit. The doctrine of the Trinity is simply the foundational claim that the persons of Father, Son and Spirit do not live in isolation, so to speak.[12] Instead, the Three give and receive existence from and to each other in a dynamic event of interdependent reciprocity. We could say that the persons exist *into* each other, generating and embracing eternal being in the endless procession and begetting of eternal life. The Christian God is the one simultaneous, harmonious and sustaining act by which the Father, Son and Spirit *are* who they are only in the one act of being interrelated. They give themselves to each other, so to speak, while making room for each other in a dynamic movement of self-emptying and self-giving, to *and* for each other; it as if they see through each other's eyes.

Yet for all its majestic beauty, the doctrine of the Trinity is also an alert. It summons Christians to the truth that God is *God* and therefore always escapes our simplistic categories of thought, wrestling free of our crude notions of Tritheism (as if we understand difference in him!) and slipping our brute concepts of monotheism (as if we understand unity in him!). Instead, the doctrine warns us that God is the eternal mystery of three persons, interrelated in perfect harmony, giving and receiving distinct identity, in a unique and dynamic divine plurality: God – we must continue to insist – is irreducibly 'one' *and* 'many' in the redefinition of both.

Now what might this account of God have to do with the reality of fresh expressions? Wary of making too quick a move from God to us – God is *not* us! – the triune nature of God does offer us a way to picture the world he has made. If God is the lively life of three persons in relation, the perfect harmony of unity and distinction, the dynamic stability of continuity and change, then might we be able to reimagine distinctions within the unity of the creation and, by extension, the Church? Could distinctions – this mixed and muddled economy we're caught up in – not be a problem that needs resolving but instead an appropriate reflection of the liveliness of God? Might the mixed economy then be seen as something to celebrate (in a non-serious way!) – that it is somehow fitting for us to *be* mixed-up in communion?

Interestingly, if we take the Christian tradition in broad scope, the case can be made that it fails to settle the paradoxes of unity and distinction, continuity and change, stability and innovation. Taken together, the Church offers a twofold pattern in which we find both moments in the paradox.[13] With Origen, for instance, the stable unity of the Christian life is underlined in the contemplative vision of ordered balance, while with someone like Gregory of Nyssa the dynamic movement of following Christ into the darkness is emphasized. It is not that we have to choose which approach is wrong and which right, just as it is not the case that we need to choose between silence and speech, negativity and positivity, individual and collective, fasting and feasting. The pairings exist in simultaneity, not producing anything by their clashing dialectic but simply together constituting an appropriate witness to the mystery that brackets and permeates our life, Father, Son and Holy Spirit. In other words, neither continuity nor change 'wins'; *life* is the mixed economy of the two in relation.

Now, if this is the case, would we be better off celebrating the mixed economy rather than expecting (hoping?) that it will be resolved sometime soon? Could inherited *and* emerging forms of Church thereby sit lightly alongside each other as they combine to point to the lively God who is Jesus Christ? Could our anxieties then lift and our life together be celebrated rather than feared?

Concluding comments

The debate about fresh expressions – as this book demonstrates – celebrates the sharing of stories and testimonies about the work of the Spirit in the life of the Church today. This chapter began by offering some anecdotal observations from such storytelling, highlighting the positive nature of interrelationship and exchange. Yet it was noted how Christians can overinflate their own importance within the mixed economy, especially when it is understood to be a temporary phenomenon from which one form of Church will emerge victorious. In light of this analysis – which I suspect is the experience of others too! – I've attempted to relocate the stories about fresh expressions in the primary story of a particular God with his creation. Two simple points have been made as a result. First, we are unnecessary creatures in whom God freely delights. When we take ourselves too seriously, we thereby fall into sin. We need to be light-hearted for God. Second, the God who freely creates us is the dynamic lively communion of Father, Son and Spirit. If God himself *is* the lively harmony of continuity and change, unity and distinction, the one and the many, might we not expect his Church to express in its own limited way these attributes too? And if this is so, should we not encourage each other to stop adjudicating between different forms of Church, and instead embrace the mixed economy as a genuinely good thing to celebrate? Should we let down our defences and instead encourage each other to discern the particular call of God on our lives and the work of God in our communities? And might it be that a playful and celebratory Church is in fact the best thing for a culture that takes itself much too seriously because it does not know God? Might a sustained and light-hearted mixed economy be the best missionary posture today?

References

Ellen T. Charry, 1997, *By The Renewing of Your Minds: The Pastoral Function of Christian Doctrine*, Oxford: Oxford University Press
Robert Jenson, 1997, *Systematic Theology*, Oxford: Oxford University Press

Notes

1 Cf. Rowan Williams; a muddled – or scruffy – economy might be closer to the truth.

2 There are too many earnest Christians around!

3 For a good introduction to systematic theology, see John Webster, 'Introduction: Systematic Theology', in John Webster, Kathryn Tanner and Iain Torrance (eds), 2007, *The Oxford Handbook of Systematic Theology*, Oxford: Oxford University Press, pp. 1–15.

4 This is not to say that the Reformation, for example, was not to do with important issues! The question would be whether Christians took themselves too seriously when they persecuted rivals such as the Anabaptists. The way of non-seriousness is the way of prophetic peace and non-violence, and though of course sin is serious, death is serious, and the cross is serious, Christ's resurrection – in part – demonstrates God's refusal to take even these too seriously!

5 We cannot invent Church from scratch. We can create new communities and seek to do wonderful things but *Church* brings with it – at least – a gospel-shaped life informed by sacraments and Scripture.

6 This sections draws on my work in the theology of sport. See, for example, L. Harvey, 'Towards a Theology of Sport: A Proposal', *Anvil* 28 (2012), forthcoming.

7 'We believe that God needs no pre-existent thing or any help in order to create, nor is creation any sort of necessary emanation from the divine substance. God creates freely "out of nothing".' *Catechism of the Catholic Church*, 296. For a full exploration of the doctrine of creation, see Colin Gunton, 1998, *The Triune Creator: A Historical and Systematic Study*, Edinburgh: Edinburgh University Press.

8 See, for example, Karl Barth, 1949, *Dogmatics in Outline*, London: SCM Press, pp. 35–64.

9 Rowan Williams, 2008, *Not Being Serious: Thomas Merton and Karl Barth*, online at http://www.archbishopofcanterbury.org/2070 [Accessed 26 January 2010].

10 See G. K. Chesterton, 2001, *St Francis of Assisi*, New York: Doubleday.

11 The only creature Francis didn't like was the ant. This is because ants work too much and don't know how to play!

12 For an introduction to these themes, see Tim Chester, 2005, *Delighting in the Trinity*, Grand Rapids and Oxford: Monarch Books.

13 See Rowan Williams, 'To Stand Where Christ Stands', in Ralph Waller and Benedicta Ward (eds), 1999, *An Introduction to Christian Spirituality*, London: SPCK, pp. 1–13.

10

The 24-7 Movement: Prayer, Justice and Social Transformation

ANDY FREEMAN

I remember that morning so well. I was at the end of three short but transforming days in Vancouver. As part of the 24-7 Prayer movement we had begun to make friends with the '614 Boiler Room' in the city, and with other groups who sought to share Christ in Vancouver. But what had attracted us was not just the beautiful city of Vancouver, but this place of crying need at its heart – the Downtown East-side.

It 5.10 a.m. and there I am awake and alert, sitting up in my couch-bed at Aaron's and Cherie's house in Vancouver. I can hear their kids beginning to stir a little and the first light of the day is coming through the curtains.

Just outside my bedroom window is the poorest postcode in North America. A social experiment gone wrong, the Downtown East-side is a place where city authorities decided to put all housing and care for the homeless and for drug addicts, and where the majority of the city's sex industry is based. Hastings, its main district, is home to 10,000 addicts; 38 per cent of its inhabitants have AIDS, 67 per cent are HIV+ and 92 per cent have Hepatitis C. This is the forgotten area of the city. If you read a tourist map, often the key to the map is placed over the Hastings area. Many guidebooks simply suggest you stay away.

But this is where I found a fresh insight into love and community; a group of friends who prayed 24-7 for four years and loved their neighbourhood in a sacrificial way that I have seldom seen.

Downtown East-side is where I met Joyce, who showed such gentle love to people in great need and asked herself daily, 'Have I loved well?' I spent a day in an unused lot of land, digging up the ground ready to plant a community garden. As I cleared hypodermic needles, condoms and broken glass ready for the topsoil of the new garden, I felt I could connect for a moment to this land, this place.

I learned something about dignity there. The inhabitants of the Downtown East-side are made in the image of God, plain and simple. These men and women look like Jesus.

I found Christ in Downtown East-side.
I found Christ as I prayed for Kathleen's broken foot.
I found Christ here as I heard new friends describe their community and the dignity and respect they have for each other.
I found Christ as Ros expressed frustration that she couldn't escape this place.
I found Christ here as I stood with a man being displaced from his home.
I found Christ here as Reg looked me in the eye and told me how stressed I looked.
I found Christ here as John asked me if I was OK.

When I first visited Vancouver, very briefly, in 2006, I only saw the vastness of this terrible social calamity. This time I saw faces. I could begin to feel the culture of the place, the atmosphere. I could sense community.

The Downtown East-side is a trial for nearly all who live there. It shouldn't be glamorized and I don't intend for a moment to do that, but what I did find in Vancouver were people who longed for life change, and who were committed in their way to those around them, who hoped for the same change. At the centre of this place was prayer.

On the Saturday night of my visit I spent a four-hour night slot in the prayer room. As I looked out of the window on the corner of Hastings, it felt right to pray. I could pray for real people I had met, pray about real problems. But I could also ask God what he was doing. I could see some moments of care as I watched a man help a woman to her feet. I could say that here was a place God had made, here were people made in the image of God.

Prayer mission and justice

The 24-7 Prayer movement operates on an axis of prayer, mission and justice. Since its inception in 1999, these three words have encapsulated what God has done among this global grassroots movement of young people, students, churches and seekers.

24-7 took inspiration from the Moravians and their inspirational leader, Count Ludwig Von Zinzendorf. Zinzendorf and the Moravians prayed continually as a community for more than a century from 1739. Their community committed to a powerful rule of life:

To be true to Christ (prayer).
To be kind to Others (justice).
To take the gospel to the nation (mission).

Over these last twelve years, 24-7 has inspired some weird and wonderful expressions of these three values:

Rescue shops in dark places such as red-light districts.
Puke-vans taking drunk clubbers home.
Transitional housing for the homeless and for drug addicts.
Christmas meals for the homeless.
Campaigns and prayer weekends about anti-human trafficking.

The list could go on and on.

It seems that when people commit to pray, God opens their eyes to the needs of the environment they live in and sends them out to make a difference. The more the 24-7 Prayer movement has prayed, the more compellingly are we sent out. It seems that this just happens. Often we fail, many times we learn, usually we find the problems and needs are well beyond us. But definitely, 24-7 can affirm that it's hard to simply pray and then do nothing at all.

The practice of justice and mercy

24-7 communities, or Boiler Rooms, operate around six values that are expressions of prayer, mission and justice.

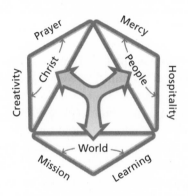

24-7 community values

One of these values is that of *mercy and justice*. Deliberately, we seek to combine the two.

The funny thing is that these two words should really clash. Mercy is about undeserved grace. In the Old Testament, the Hebrew word *hesed* is often used, referring to right conduct towards fellow men or loyalty to the Lord, or both. In essence, what God requires from us is to love each other and him. Sometimes *hesed* is actually translated 'love' (for example, Hosea 6.4). The dictionary definition of mercy includes 'forbearance towards one who is in one's power; a forgiving disposition; compassion for the unfortunate' (Chambers, 1998).

The understanding of acting justly in Israelite law was to not mistreat the alien, widows and orphans. God declared that if 'they cry out to me, I will certainly hear their cry' (Exod. 22. 22–27). In the Bible, justice shouldn't be denied (see Exod. 23.6) or perverted (see Lev. 19.15). To deliver justice requires wisdom (see 1 Kings 3.28) and discernment (see 1 Kings 3.11). Justice is a way God acts towards mankind, and the cross is the ultimate demonstration (see Rom. 3.25). Justice is also something demanded of us: 'Follow justice and justice alone' (Deut. 16.20).

But mercy and justice are often found together in Scripture. In God's call through Zechariah, mirroring a similar message in Micah, mercy and justice are non-negotiable to obey God:

> This is what the LORD Almighty says: 'Administer true justice; show mercy and compassion to one another. Do not oppress the widow or the fatherless, the alien or the poor. In your hearts do not think evil of each other.' (Zech. 7.9–10)

Mercy and justice also combine explosively at the cross, where Jesus died in our place and expressed the love and forgiveness of God. True mercy only exists in tandem with just actions. True justice is only expressed when given in a merciful way.

Sometimes justice and mercy challenge us because they seem like magnets repelling each other. We meet people in great need who ask for mercy, yet we ask questions of justice. Is this fair? Do they deserve different treatment than others?

Many questioned the Boiler Room's involvement with the excluded teenagers of my home town of Reading, Berkshire. When another wallet was stolen we asked ourselves: Did we invite trouble when we made friends with these kids? And who will pay for that broken window? Sometimes situations of injustice shattered us and all we wanted to do was give up. Yet the life and death of Jesus spurred us on. At the cross, mercy and justice came together. There, justice was done for our sin and the mercy of God embraced us 'while we were still sinners' (see Rom. 5.8).

In J. R. R. Tolkien's *The Lord of the Rings*, the relationship between Gollum and Frodo highlights the tension of justice and mercy. Gollum was a murderer, and Frodo's best friend Sam knew he would kill again, given half a chance. Justice demanded Gollum's death, but mercy enabled Frodo to see from the perspective of his own burden of the ring. He knew it was the ring that had warped Gollum; and he knew that he could easily walk down that path too. He remembered the words of Gandalf:

> Deserves death! I daresay he does. Many that live deserve death. And some that die deserve life. Can you give that to them? Then be not too eager to deal out death in the name of justice, fearing for your own safety. Even the wise cannot see all ends. (Tolkien, 1968, p. 380)

The mercy and justice that beats at the heart of God must become our heartbeat. He has shown us mercy; therefore we should lay down our own lives (see Rom. 12.1). If justice is the foundation of God's throne, it must be the foundation of our lives too (see Zech. 7.9). Will God be merciful to us if we fail to show mercy to others (see Matt. 5.7, James 2.13)? What justice can we expect if we fail to show justice to others (see Isa. 58)? Mercy and justice flow through the character of God. They should flow through us too.

Made in his image

> God created man in his own image, in the image of God he created him; male and female he created them. (Gen. 1.27)

During my time with the 614 Boiler Room in Vancouver I re-thought my whole understanding of this verse. Consider it for a moment. The people we sit next to in the train, the people who live next door: they're made in the image of God, and the love he has for them is immense. Each one is of value to God (see Ps. 139). He died for us out of love (see John 3.16), he delights in each of us (see Zeph. 3.17).

24-7 Boiler Rooms are committed to welcoming the poor and those in need. This isn't simply about programmes or projects. Ultimately, people are invited to be part of our community. In 2009, when our community in Reading wanted to celebrate Christmas, we didn't feel right not to include our friends who are street-sleepers in the area. The only thing to do was bring our dinner and presents out on to the street and spend time together.

Andrea, part of our community, recorded it like this:

Gabriel was in his usual spot at the top of the alley, Christmas lights lined the ceiling of the alleyway. He played a tune for us, Bob Dylan's 'Knock, knock knocking on heaven's door' and we sang along. A few moments later some drunken lads coming up the alley started singing Oasis' 'Wonderwall' and Gabriel changes track mid-song and starts to play it. There's a beautiful moment when we're all singing the song, it feels kinda special, a bundle of lives that would not in normal circumstances have come together are thrown together and find some commonality in that moment on a street corner. The drunken lads throw him some coins and move on their way ...

We gave him some Christmas presents from our little community, he smiled shyly, saying: 'Thank you, you're so kind' and tucked them inside his jacket. He starts to play again ...

We move on our way to meet our friend Reid. We'd seen him earlier in the week and he told us where we would find him tonight. If I'm honest I was hoping we wouldn't find him. It was a freezing cold night, snow was thick on the ground, I couldn't feel my toes and I'd only been out and hour or so. He would be freezing. I was hoping he'd be somewhere else, somewhere warm. But he was there, right where he said he would be.

We sat with him on the street and shared a mince pie and hot chocolate. He opened a couple of his presents, some useful ones, gloves and warm socks. Thanking us, he said he'd save the rest as it would be nice to have something to open on Christmas Day. As we said our goodbyes and wandered on our way, it was with some sadness. I wish we could do something more ... I wish we could take him home with us.[1]

This truth means that we must treat all persons with respect and dignity. God does, and so should we. God's image imprinted on each individual is the starting point for a practice of mercy and justice. Jesus declared:

For I was hungry and you gave me something to eat, I was thirsty and you gave me something to drink, I was a stranger and you invited me in, I needed clothes and you clothed me, I was sick and you looked after me, I was in prison and you came to visit me. (Matt. 25.35–36)

About a month after we opened the Reading Boiler Room (2001), we allowed the building to be used for a Saturday prayer gathering. Intercessors and church people gathered to pray for the young. They called out to God that the young would feel drawn to church, that the Church would reach out to them. At the end of the prayer meeting, many of the people approached me to complain about the Goths and Skaters hanging out in the building. They complained that they couldn't park their cars because young people were skateboarding in the parking lot. They complained about the noise from the young people in the prayer room. They complained about the kids for whom they were praying.

The teenagers of the Forbury, a small park in central Reading, were not deserving in the eyes of those who prayed for them that day, but the mercy and justice of the God who had designed them in his own image was already at work. If we want to follow God's lead, we must remember that none of us deserves God's mercy, and all of us can receive it.

The Church: reshaping the existing order

The method of the Church's impact on society at large should be twofold. First, the Church must announce Christian principles and point out where the existing social order is in conflict with them. Second, it must then pass on to Christian citizens, acting in their civic capacities, the task of reshaping the existing order in closer conformity to its principles (Temple, 1976, p. 233).

William Temple, Archbishop of York, wrote this challenge in the 1940s to a Church that played a major role in society and social change. Sixty years later, economic and social injustices are often hidden and those in need are those outside of the system's reach. Now as much as ever, the Church is called to be an agent of change.

> Say no to wrong. Learn to do good. Work for justice. Help the down-and-out. Stand up for the homeless. Go to bat for the defenseless (Isa. 1.13–17, *The Message*).

This justice mandate must be expressed both locally and globally. God's Spirit might prompt us to show mercy through practical care for prostitutes who walk our streets at night, and may prompt us to oppose the injustices at the root of prostitution. But the reality is that we live in a time of global injustice, where the needy often finance the growth and success of the richer nations. In these times of unprecedented global connections, the Church must show mercy and act justly both at home and abroad.

In its own small way, the 24-7 Prayer movement has sought to connect prayer with a desire for justice and a commitment to transforming society. We've tried to do this in a few simple ways.

1 Identification: standing with the wronged

To act justly means we should be angered by injustice. To show mercy means to stand with people who are wronged. Jesus walked out to John in the desert to be baptized. John couldn't believe that the Messiah was coming to him! 'I need to be baptized by you, and do you come to me?' (Matt. 3.14). But Jesus insisted, 'to fulfil all righteousness'; to be obedient to his Father, to fulfil prophecy, but also to identify, to stand with the people he had come to save.

Jesus 'did not consider equality with God something to be grasped' (Phil. 2.6), and he gave up his glory to become flesh and blood and move into the neighbourhood (see John 1.14). John baptized for the forgiveness of sins, yet here was the sinless Christ, waiting in line to be baptized. Why? Because he chose to stand with humanity, with the lost, with the poor, with the wronged. He chose to stand with the people. Jesus was a friend of the poor, and he hung out with sinners and tax collectors. He did not come to 'call the righteous, but sinners' (Matt. 9.13). He had compassion on the crowds, cared for the outcasts, had tea with a tax collector and allowed himself to be anointed by a prostitute. He stood up to the Pharisees when they blocked the door to God. He stood for the left out and left behind, and we must do the same. When we seek to identify with those in need, we can do so combining prayer and action.

Intercessory prayer needs a sense of personal identification to be effective. We are standing in the middle, on behalf of others, bringing them to God. We can do this without connection, simply going through the motions. But when we come with understanding and compassion, the prayers change and become deeper. We will also invariably act.

Our model for intercession is Jesus, who intercedes for us with the Father (Isa. 53.12; Rom. 8.26–27). Jesus' path of intercession is incarnational – it is present with us – he understands our challenges, our weaknesses. Can we tie together intercessory prayer and taking action? Can we stand with the poor with our prayers and with our deeds?

2 Being responsive

Each Boiler Room asks itself several questions: How will the poor be affected by what we do today? Will they be welcome? Will our choices and decisions affect them? Will that effect be positive or negative? Sometimes the simplest thing we can do is ask 'How can we help?' Issues such as poverty can seem enormous, yet simple steps of care and compassion, simple prayers to a loving God – they can change the world.

> Like slavery and apartheid, poverty is not natural. It is manmade and it can be overcome.
> (Nelson Mandela speaking at the Make Poverty History Launch in Trafalgar Square, February 2005)

3 Keeping it simple

Many Boiler Rooms live out this part of the Rule simply by responding to needs that turn up, whether with disadvantaged children in Kansas City, excluded young people in Skopje or families in need in Guildford. Boiler Rooms try to help when they're asked.

This can be done in partnership with other organizations. If you feel challenged to feed the homeless in your community, look around you. Someone is already doing it, and perhaps you can partner and support rather than reinvent the wheel. Why not call your local homeless shelter and ask how you can help? It's tempting to start a project ourselves, but sometimes the biggest solution we can bring to the problem is our time. Sometimes, the last thing we need is the limelight.

> Nurture a love to do good things in secret ... be content to go without praise. (Jeremy Taylor, seventeenth-century English clergyman, 2006)

4 Responding with prayer

Sometimes we can't fix the problem, but our prayers can move mountains. Our actions must be accompanied by passionate and persistent prayer. We must live as though it all depends on us, and pray as though it all depends on God.

> And will not God bring about justice for his chosen ones, who cry out to him day and night? (Luke 18.7)

What is God Doing?

In 2011, the 24-7 Prayer movement spent a month praying about the HIV/AIDS crisis. It's anticipated that 33 million people have the virus. HIV is one of those crippling issues that are the knot at the centre of so many social problems in the developing world. Surely this is just too big a problem?

For many in 24-7, HIV has become one of those issues that we know we need to pray for. I regularly ask God to provide a cure for HIV. Surely the God who created the world, the God who designed DNA, the God who knits us together – surely he can help doctors and scientists exploring a vaccine? Surely prayer can change this?

For myself, a passion to pray for HIV hasn't come from a charity's work, from a TV programme or from a campaign. It's been the voice of God speaking into my own feeble soul. It's been as I prayed, and as God began to beckon me over to him, as he began to show me something of his heart, his mission, his compassion.

When we seek to be merciful, when we seek justice for others, when we fight for social transformation, we are not beginning a new journey. Instead we join in the ongoing mission of God. When we pray we can begin by asking God, 'What are you doing in our world?'

Mission is not primarily an activity of the Church, but an attribute of God. God is a missionary God. (Bosch, 1991, pp. 389–90)

References

David J. Bosch, 1991, *Transforming Mission*, Maryknoll: Orbis Books
Chambers English Dictionary, 1998, Edinburgh: Chambers
Jeremy Taylor, 2006, *The Rule and Exercises of Holy Living*, Whitefish, MT: Kessinger Publishing
William Temple, 1976, *Christianity and the Social Order*, London: Shephard-Walwyn Ltd
J. R. R. Tolkien, 1968, *The Lord of the Rings*, London: Allen & Unwin

Note

1 http://uk.24-7prayer.com/stories/a-reconcile-christmas-reading-part-2/

11

Campus Context

MIKE ANGELL

A collection of students at the University of California had a hunch. Over the two years I worked for the Episcopal Church as chaplain to the San Diego UC campus, I heard hundreds of students explain their intuition: 'I just know the world shouldn't be like this.' 'I have a feeling that we could live more justly, treat one another better.' Over and over I listened as college students described their sense that the world needed change, that something better was possible. I had learned to name that hunch for myself: to talk about the Kingdom of God as the centre of Christian life. Could our campus ministry help these students name the hunch as well?

I spent time listening largely because there were so few Episcopalians on campus. I had been hired as the pastoral presence for the Episcopal Church to the 29,000-member university. In those days with a Facebook search you could see how many students identified with your religious group on campus. The number of Episcopalians: four. There were an additional two international students who identified as Anglican, which brought the total to six. University ministry has traditionally been thought of as chaplaincy: the campus minister serves the needs of those on campus already identifying with their tradition. If I spent an hour a week with each Anglican student, I would have had 34 spare hours out of my 40-hour work week. I started listening to other students and started hearing about this hunch.

Most students with whom I spoke had no religious experience, and few had ever been inside a church building (save for the occasional wedding or funeral). Their parents or grand-parents had walked away from Church and had not felt the need to bring their child up with any sort of faith. Some students saw the Church as problematic, as an institution that contributed to exclusion and hatred in the world. More were indifferent. They didn't have any impression of faith.

This was tricky for a religious professional. Many of these students really didn't know what to do when they encountered a 'campus minister'. They lacked spiritual and religious vocabulary. One of them kept referring to me as an 'Episcopopple'. Students worried about the words they used in front of me. Sometimes, in spite of my protests, they treated me like a sort of moral police officer, unnecessarily apologizing for the occasional curse word or how they spent a weekend. So many students seemed nervous around me. I was nervous too. Often I didn't know what to say as a chaplain to people without faith, but I provided free coffee and listened. We shared a hunger for justice. Some students would even describe their hunch that the world could be better as a sense of vocation. They said they felt called to live their life differently, even as they said they didn't have a name for whatever was calling them.

When I came to work at UCSD, I had just come back from my own response to such a sense of call. Unlike these students, I grew up in church. My mother is an Episcopal priest in Colorado. I had voluntarily gone to evangelical youth groups with friends in high school, and had chosen to attend a Roman Catholic University to study theology. Arriving at college I was a church rat but, like the students at UCSD, had never framed my sense of social justice with questions of faith. That all changed as I began to study the liberation theology of Latin America. In particular I was inspired by the story of the Church in El Salvador. Led by the martyred Bishop Óscar Romero, priests, nuns, theologians and lay people had stepped out for justice. They centred their faith in Jesus' proclamation of the Kingdom of God, understanding Christ's offer of salvation to mean that God promised a better future, and that faith demanded and directed action for justice.

Before encountering this understanding of the Christian

message, I had always understood God's will to involve some vague notion of love for those around us and good behaviour. Listening to the stories of the Church in Central America, I encountered Christians who believed there was nothing vague about Christian love. Loving action was concrete, and worked that every person might be fully alive. As a college student, I began to get involved at my university in action for social justice and simultaneously more deeply involved in the life of our college chapel. I continued to encounter a spirituality that was centred in the Kingdom of God.

While I had never really walked away from the Church, this vision of the Kingdom of God brought my faith to life. It brought a sense of urgency to prayer and action. More importantly, it gave words to my sense that the world was not as it should be. The vision of the Kingdom of God stood up against a broken and divided world, and it haunted me. The more I read and listened, the more my internal hunch called my attention. Not only did I know that the world wasn't as it should be, I knew I had to do something about it. That my faith demanded action was more than an intellectual belief. Something in me knew deeply, palpably, that the world needed to change, and I needed to be part of it.

I spent a year after university chasing that dream to Honduras. I signed up with the Episcopal Church's Young Adult Service Corps to work at an orphanage in Tegucigalpa. Living in Latin America was humbling. At first I was frustrated that the inbreaking of the Kingdom of God didn't happen immediately when I set foot in the slums. My imagination stopped short of expecting the Risen Lord to meet my plane, but I fully expected to make a measurable and concrete difference. Maddeningly, no big change happened because I went to Honduras. I didn't save anyone's life or change the course of the nation. But that hunch I had kept growing. The hunger I felt for justice became a sense of invitation to collaborate with God over a lifetime.

After my year in Honduras, I began the work as Episcopal campus missioner at UCSD. We began by exploring a possible justice-oriented trip to El Salvador, and as momentum built for the chaplaincy, we found that it was far easier to invite a friend along to feed someone, to engage a question of justice, than it was to invite them to a worship service. It was easier to make the invitation, and people were more likely to accept, but this was slippery ground. We didn't want to be seen simply as a 'social service club'. We needed to have a conversation about why we were engaging in this work, and that was nerve-wracking. We didn't want to drive people away. After stumbling through the first conversations, we surprisingly found that most students were interested to hear about why a faith group was engaged in justice. They were hungry, not just for an opportunity to serve, but for a vision to fill in their hunch about the way the world should be.

Margo started at the edges of our little band. She was friends with Elisse, a liberal Catholic student who had been helping lead our trips to an orphanage in Tijuana. Margo grew up in a very secular family. Though she went to Catholic High School and said she was 'comfortable around people of faith', she had always thought of herself as categorically 'not religious'. Margo began spending time with us because Elisse had asked her to come along on our Spring Break trip to El Salvador.

I made a point of meeting with and interviewing every appli-cant for our trips. Talking with Margo was a joy. When we met, she seemed a bit unsure, but as we talked she opened up. Margo has a vibrant mind and a great sense of humour. She described her desire to come to El Salvador negatively: she did not want to spend her week-long vacation partying on a beach somewhere. She felt the time could be better used – given away, even. She said she wanted to know better what life was like for people living in poverty, and she wanted to know how she could be part of a change.

During our week in El Salvador, I was consistently impressed by Margo's openness. El Salvador is decidedly not secularized, and we were hosted by the Anglican Church. People talked openly and regularly about their faith, and how God had brought them through the difficulties of the war. If you ask someone on the street how they are feeling, they are likely to say, 'Thanks be to God, I am well.' I was nervous for Margo, but she was not closed to all this discussion of religion. Margo embraced the experiences and stories she heard. In the evenings, we often gathered around for Evening Prayer and reflection. While she says she mentally translated our word 'prayer' into 'meditation', Margo engaged in these conversations deeply. She says that it was important that she felt safe, not pressured to believe or threatened with some consequence for a lack of faith.

One night, after we had visited the University of Central America where six Jesuit theologians and their housekeepers had been martyred, Margo felt safe to ask questions about faith and God. Such a moment had never really happened for her before. I interviewed Margo recently as I prepared to write this piece. As we talked on the phone a gravity developed as she described that night as, the 'two hours of my life when I've been most communicative about faith'. Margo does not see herself as a 'seeker', but that night, even if just for a hesitant moment, she was 'seeking'. Working collaboratively alongside Christians for a shared vision of the world was an entry point for her.

Margo still does not identify as religious, but she says encountering our group and working with us in El Salvador opened her up to a new perspective on faith. She continues to search for ways to participate in action for justice, and saw her time with us in El Salvador as an important benchmark in shaping her vision of the way the world could be. Margo doesn't use Christian language, but her hunch led her to reach out beyond her comfort zone. She still identifies, with her family of origin, as 'non-religious', but for Margo the Kingdom of God was good news.

The Kingdom of God isn't a simple formula. It can't be boiled down to a programme of social service that will win converts for your church or student group. The Episcopal chaplaincy at UCSD wasn't the only game in town. The University of California, San Diego, played host to two dozen or so para-church ministries, non- or multi-denominational entities like Campus Crusade for Christ. Many groups were aggressive in their stance towards non-believers, preaching a 'convert or burn' theology that created an aversion for many students towards Christian groups.

Some of these groups were less virulent. InterVarsity Christian Fellowship had caught on to 'the hunch' as well. Their ministry often engaged questions of justice. For an entire week InterVarsity constructed a hundred meter long tent in the middle of campus that was staffed 24 hours a day. A participant entered the tent, received a headset, and headed down one of three hallways through the structure. Each different pathway told a moving human story of someone living with AIDS in Africa. Pictures, video, audio, and even household objects captured the person's daily life. The tent did a great job connecting a participant with the justice concerns around HIV, but at the other end of the tent, the whole narrative shifted. Each person was greeted at the end of their experience by a student who asked if what they saw in the tent made them want to commit their life to Jesus. It was incongruous. Many of the students I spoke with felt the whole experience to be an elaborate trick, a play on the emotions to render a participant vulnerable to making a big life decision. One night as the Episcopal group gathered for dinner, a student shared with me that she felt InterVarsity 'might as well be selling condo time-shares'. In the Episcopal chaplaincy, we didn't think direct confrontation was the way to encounter big questions of faith. Surely Inter-Varsity had a bigger tally of 'converts' at the end of the year, but we weren't really counting that way.

For us, crossing international borders seemed an appropriate place to invite the spiritual seekers. One student, Samantha, found her faith again over a series of trips to an Episcopal orphanage in Tijuana. Samantha's family had attended church when she was a little girl, but when she was twelve her father became embroiled in social conflict in the congregation. The melodrama proved too much, and she decided she did not want to be part of Church anymore. Arriving at college, Samantha felt her spiritual life needed support. The next year we hired a musician for our worship services who happened to be Samantha's friend. When he invited her to come to worship, she was shy. Then she came to Dorcas House.

Every month our group drove 25 minutes from the University of California campus to the front gate of Dorcas House in

Tijuana, Mexico. Each time when we arrived, the children surrounded us, and the play started immediately. These 45 or so
children, aged between four and 15, really did not care whether
our group spoke Spanish. There was soccer to play, books to
be coloured in, puzzles to solve, and dancing to do. Samantha
says that what really amazed her was that the kids remembered
several of the students' names. Because we came regularly, relationships developed. Samantha was moved by the passion she
saw in the other UCSD students, and their sense that they came
because of their faith.

It takes 25 minutes to get to Dorcas House; it can take hours
to make it through the US Immigration control line to get
back. As our van waited in line to cross the border, we talked
about the implications of spending a day in Tijuana with the
kids. Samantha, who had been a bit quiet in our group, came
alive, talking about seeing Christ in children who she otherwise would never have met. In the months to come, Samantha
would begin to take a leadership role in organizing our trips to
Dorcas, and the kids would start to call her by name.

All of us were stretched by the encounters we had in Mexico
and El Salvador. We stepped over exterior and interior human
boundaries, set up to set us apart from one another. This
wasn't easy work. For those of us who had grown up Christian, stepping into a foreign country, getting to know a child
whose story was radically different from ours, stretched us. For
those who did not name a faith tradition, spending this much
time with people who engaged in 'God talk' brought them out
of their comfort zone. What we shared was a hunch that something about reaching out in this way was necessary for our
world, for us to be who we are called to be. Crossing borders
together, we shared glimpses of what a wandering Galilean
called the Kingdom of God.

12

Fresh Expressions and Catholic Social Justice Teaching

DAMIAN FEENEY

Introduction

In a period of numerical decline in church attendance, and therefore of constrained resources, it is tempting to see anything with a 'Mission' label purely as an answer to that decline. Even in relatively enlightened contexts the assumption that the fresh expressions movement has, as its principal aim, the mere goal of increasing numerical attendance and membership, can be hard to shift. To be sure, it has taken quite some time to usher in the view of a 'mixed economy' Church, as expounded by Rowan Williams and others.[1] This can have the effect of 'masking' a more comprehensive and healthy view of the mission of the Church.

As a member of the working party that contributed towards *Mission-shaped Church*, I had the privilege of speaking at a great many gatherings at diocesan, deanery and parochial levels following the launch of the report in 2004. The presentations always included a mention of the five marks of mission, adopted by the Anglican Communion worldwide. These marks are:

- To proclaim the good news of the kingdom.
- To teach, baptize and nurture new believers.
- To respond to human need by loving service.

- To seek to transform unjust structures of society.
- To strive to safeguard the integrity of creation and sustain and renew the life of the earth.

(Anglican Church Communion, 1984, p. 49; 1990, p. 101)

My concern in this chapter is to argue for a more balanced view of the formation of fresh expressions of Church, and a modelling of such a view from which both 'inherited' and 'emerging' church can learn, without distinction. Each of the five marks of mission outlined above has an aspect concerning the social teachings of Jesus, but perhaps a particular focus can be discerned in marks 3–5. This emphasis on social justice has been echoed by, and characteristic of, the Roman Catholic Church since the end of the nineteenth century, and has found particular focus since the Second Vatican Council in recent encyclicals during the papacies of John Paul II and Benedict XVI. Both as a body of teaching and as historical legacy, the encyclicals and statements encompassed are remarkable as a reflection of the times in which they were written and as a prophetic witness to the Kingdom of God. In totality they represent an unsurpassed attempt to recall the Church to considerations of social and ethical justice across a bewildering and complex period of world history. Moreover, as a body of teaching its influence extends beyond the denominational boundaries of Roman Catholicism itself, influencing a wide range of Christian traditions.

This chapter will, inevitably, be more about advocacy than analysis. The very concept of the mixed economy Church is young, as are the fledgling communities that have emerged, both prior to and following the publication of the report. I wish to suggest that the ethos of fresh expressions could and should create opportunities and models that render more explicit the demands of service and social justice that are integral to the gospel. I will also argue that a church concerned for such teaching needs to place the Eucharist at the centre of its missional life. Of course, such specific remits can never be the sole reason for being; nor is this to suggest that such a priority is not entirely appropriate in the life of a mainstream parish.

The body of Catholic social teaching

Specifically, the documents in question range from Pope Leo XIII's 1891 encyclical *Rerum Novarum* to Benedict XVI's *Caritas in Veritate* (2009).[2] Each document is a creation of its time, and together they provide an interesting history of social and ecclesial change and development through the twentieth century. They may be distilled into ten major themes, which are:[3]

• The dignity and holiness of the human person.
• Common good and community.
• Option for the poor.
• Rights and responsibilities.
• The role of government and subsidiarity.
• Economic justice.
• Stewardship of God's creation.
• Promotion of peace and disarmament.
• Participation.
• Global solidarity and development.

This list, compiled from the original documents by the St Paul and Minneapolis Center for Social Justice, indicates something of the scope of this agenda. Each principle is a huge subject on its own; perhaps for those wishing to explore this area of mission, the above may act as a checklist or an inspiration for discernment.

There are two ways in which such concepts should impact upon the discernment, formation and operation of fresh expressions of Church. First, there is the issue of formation: how new Christian communities are formed, in such a way that the values of the kingdom are rendered explicit and, in the best sense, institutional. To what are new expressions of Church seeking to respond? Second, there is the issue of what is proclaimed, taught and lived by the Christian community. A community of Christian believers that transforms and convicts those in contact with it has always been the most effective agent of evangelism. As Newbigin observed, 'the only answer, the only hermeneutic of the gospel, is a congregation of men and women who believe it and live by it' (1989, p. 227).

It is tempting to see the needs and requirements of social justice in the life of the ecclesial community as somehow secondary to the business of worship and pastoral care. In truth, the multifaceted nature of church life demands coherence in language, praxis and approach. Paying attention to the imperatives of the words of Jesus means finding ways of enabling his words and actions to shine through our own. Finding richer, more effective ways of expressing the priorities of the kingdom throughout the life of the Church is a key task, which is not merely pertinent to a holistic view of mission but actually plays its part in the more focused business of evangelization or evangelism.[4] Dulles makes this point when he says:

> By promoting right order of values in their earthly activities, Christians practice faithfulness to the gospel and win respect for it. Allowing their whole lives to be permeated by the spirit of the beatitudes, they promote justice and charity in society. (2009, p. 12)

Any first glance at the list of principles given above might focus on the global nature of those I have outlined. Issues of government, economic justice and disarmament may seem to be issues 'beyond the scope' of the local church. Yet there are invariably local manifestations of global issues that affect small groups of people and for which a voice is needed. Additionally, global issues are global precisely because they affect everyone. Too often we are 'parochial' in the worst and most pejorative sense – seeing only those things our eyes can see, or that we want to see, and failing to recognize our commitment to our brothers and sisters in need, merely because they are on our television screens and not living next door. Fresh expressions, it seems, are formed to fill spaces in provision, to attempt to reach groups of people who remain untouched by mainstream parochial life. Fresh expressions that form in response to a specific social issue or context may well be in a position to raise awareness and respond to such issues more directly.

Concerns and criticisms

Is it possible that the fundamental ethos of fresh expressions militates against this type of mission? Certainly, criticisms of this type have been levelled at *Mission-shaped Church* by Hull and others (Hull, 2006, pp. 12–15). The creation of diverse forms of Church – especially in networks – encourages a formation of congregations along the lines of self-selecting social grouping, which is at odds with the spirit of the gospel. Hull's criticism lies in what he sees as the inappropriate use of the 'Homogenous Unit Principle' of Donald McGavran (1955) – a principle coming out of McGavran's experiences in India, where social and, specifically, caste issues proved problematic to a more integrated model of church life. This theme has been recently developed by Davison and Milbank in what they refer to as 'The Flight to Segregation' (2010, Ch. 4). One response to this argument can be made by considering the model offered by many parish communities on the 'other side' of the mixed economy. While the Anglican parochial system is rooted in the service of a geographical area by a specific church community or communities, it would be a mistake to suppose that to be the end of the story. People choose where they 'go to church'. Factors of tradition, churchmanship, family ties in another community as well as the increased mobility of a proportion of society are all factors that may be cited as promoting eclecticism. These issues are alive and well on both sides of the mixed economy, and it is a rare parish church indeed that does not have some eclectic factor within its profile. Bishop Cray makes this point in his response to Davison and Milbank:

> Many parish congregations were already more or less homogeneous units, in other words groups made up of a single people type or culture, and it [Church growth thinking] opened the way to expanding their reach by engaging with groups which had been untouched.[5]

That is not, however, to excuse what can be read as the exacerbation of this factor in the founding ethos of fresh expressions, and perhaps it is in the modelling of a social agenda that such issues can be brought to the light, reflected upon, and addressed within the local church. Ultimately people choose which faith community to belong to, and for a host of diverse reasons; perhaps the provision of further diversity will broaden and enhance that choice.

A further factor in this regard lies in the encouragement, within church growth models across the mixed economy, of basing mission and outreach events upon culturally apposite themes, designed to encourage people in a community to engage with the gospel via the channel of a specific interest. This strategy is, for example, a key component in the teaching material of the 'Leading your Church into Growth' movement – teaching aimed squarely at parish-based mission.[6] So a parish where there is a keen gardening culture might offer some sort of gardening event to persuade the local community to make connections between something very close to them and the gospel of Jesus Christ. Such strategies touch people within specific interest groups, and seek to incorporate those people into the life of the wider parish. This, no doubt, segregates people in a similar way. This is an important distinction within the mixed economy, since that sense of incorporation within a parish community should ultimately lead to a breaking down of the barriers. It is therefore important to distinguish between genuine fresh expressions of Church and what might be termed 'refreshed expressions'.[7] The latter is a more appropriate term for outreach events and new communities that flow from the life of the mainstream parish and that may be remodelled or rebranded in order to appeal to a wider constituency of parishioners. These types of expression are not as prey to Hull's 'homogeneity' argument, but nonetheless involve interest groups of one kind or another, where group membership can be determined by factors of age, gender or interest. In addition, and as Cray points out, the majority of fresh expressions at this time are flowing from the life of parishes. Nevertheless, the question remains: can fresh expressions be places where personal identities and attitudes are challenged and transformed, rather than merely affirmed and accepted?

The question of eclecticism remains as an issue throughout the whole Church.

Fresh expressions of Church were never intended to be a 'window box'[8] for the ultimate transplanting of seedlings into more mature forms of Church. Some are invariably transitory, while others will find greater stability. There is, of course, no such thing as a permanently stable local church, inherited or otherwise. The ethos of the mixed economy presupposes the integrity of a diversity of expressions alongside those within the inherited Church, principally within parishes. If that is so, it seems fair to suggest that fresh expressions might be lighter on their feet than the mainstream inherited Church is sometimes able to be. One of the challenges the Church might throw down to the fresh expressions movement is to be yet more responsive to social and economic issues. The only way to refute Hull's arguments concerning the social exclusion implied by eclecticism is for fresh expressions communities to live lives that transform local communities, to be a voice for people who are unable to express needs and concerns, and to express something of the advocacy of Jesus Christ in the political sphere. That has to find concrete expression in (among other things) aiming to lift people out of material poverty.

It seems clear that for fresh expressions of Church to model adequately the gospel concerns of social justice, a reappraisal of the segregation question needs to take place. Notwithstanding the desirability of promoting a mixed economy, it is problematic to create new forms of Church that seem to institutionalize segregation. Of course this was never the intention of the report, but calls into question the matter of strategic process in mission that lies at the heart of our understanding of call, proclamation and incorporation. Over a period of time it may become apparent as to whether fresh expressions enable the kind of action and reflection that enables barriers to be broken down rather than built up.[9]

Theoretically it ought to be possible to reflect upon models of Church that strengthen the hand of social issues and apply them to fresh expressions. This is rendered more complex by the sheer diversity of expression that *Mission-shaped Church* discovered in the ten years since the report *Breaking New Ground* (Archbishop's Council, 1994) was published, and that continues to develop at a bewildering pace. In this diversity they model one of the more obvious traits of postmodernism. Does this mean that fresh expressions will be more effective in speaking to contemporary culture, or is there a danger that such expressions will lose their sense of rootedness in tradition?

Most recently, in the encyclical *Deus Caritas Est*, Pope Benedict develops a theme that found further expression during his 2010 visit to the British Isles – that of the dialogue between faith and reason (para. 28a, p. 31). For some this merely represented the dialogue between faith groups and political structures in a national discourse. In time, the Pope's words may seem yet more instructive in the lives of local churches and initiatives. The encyclical's words are most instructive when we consider issues such as the Church's role in political advocacy: 'The Church wishes to help form consciences in political life and to stimulate greater insight into the authentic requirements of justice as well as greater readiness to act accordingly' (2006, p. 31).

The forming of conscience, the stimulation of insight, the readiness to act. This summary could be taken as a template for any local church in mission. Church communities that are formed around specific issues should be more ready to respond, able to operate with a lighter touch, and able to offer authentic insights to those whose task it is to make political decisions. Church communities that are seen to work for the good of the whole community, campaigning in significant local and global issues, contribute to the ongoing debate about the *value* of the presence and role of the Church, and are part of a wordless yet important response to debates about the role of faith in civic and public life. Might we find such churches among fresh expressions?

The Eucharist

It would be impossible to address this subject and not to refer to the ground of activity that every report and encyclical assumes as the core activity of the Church – that of the celebration of the Eucharist. The report *Mission-shaped Church* treated the Eucharist as a core activity of the inherited Church, and something of a 'barrier' for any new expression of Church.

> Churches are eucharistic communities, irrespective of their church tradition, or the frequency of eucharistic worship. The Eucharist lies at the heart of Christian life. It is the act of worship (including the Ministry of the Word) in which the central core of the biblical gospel is retold and re-enacted. New expressions of church may raise practical difficulties about authorized ministry, but, if they are to endure, they must celebrate the Eucharist. (2004, p. 101)

Here the Eucharist is seen as a characteristic of the Church, central to its life, even if the language employed implies that it is an obstacle to be overcome rather than a gift to be embraced. It is perceived that however 'central' the Eucharist may be in the life of the Church, it is somehow restricted in its efficacy as an evangelistic strategy by a multitude of issues. These issues include the question of appropriate ordained leadership, and of who may or may not receive the Eucharist, and therefore raise questions of levels of participation and accessibility. There is also an important sense in which the Eucharist is perceived within tradition to be the culmination of a process of catechesis and initiation rather than a place where *initial* encounters with God in Christ are possible.

That said, important questions for fresh expressions that wish to engage authentically with social justice issues are raised by their liturgies, which are the embodiment of the life of the ecclesial community, as well as an expression of the values of the kingdom; the Eucharist is unique in this regard. Nothing can replicate or replace its effect, since it is supremely God's action for his people. In another time and context, Austin Farrer wrote of the Eucharist, 'This sacrament is not a special part of our religion, it *is* just our religion, sacramentally enacted' (1952, p. 58).

Roman Catholic theologians since the Second Vatican Council have gone further, stating boldly that the Eucharist is integral to the very identity of Church. The then Cardinal Ratzinger makes this point in emphasizing the *distinctive* nature of ecclesial identity:

> The Church is not merely an external society of believers; by her nature, she is a liturgical community; she is most truly church when she celebrates the Eucharist and makes present the redemptive love of Jesus Christ ... (Ratzinger, 1987, p. 50)

Regardless of tradition, and recognizing the strong statement from the report quoted above, a key question for fresh expressions of all shapes and sizes will not be *whether*, but rather *when and how*. Apart from any other consideration, this is a specific issue for Ordained Pioneer Ministry training, taking place as it does within a mixed-mode context where leadership may be able to grow alongside (and integrally with) the fresh expression served.

There is a danger that neglect in this area can lead to a disembodiment of such values wherever the sacramental economy in general, and the Eucharist in particular, is relegated from its central place within Christian life and worship. The ways in which the Eucharist embodies and expresses the core gospel values is encapsulated by Hauerwas and Wells, whose *Blackwell Companion to Christian Ethics* structurally reflects the shape and pattern of the Eucharist, as an attempt to reinforce in our understanding the intimate and profound relationship between liturgy and the ethical outworking of Christian doctrine. Can fresh expressions find an appropriate and creative balance between creative innovation and the ecclesial rootedness of the Eucharist?

The ancient phrase *lex orandi, lex credendi* is seen as a summary of this relationship – that as the church worships, so the church believes.[10] As Angela Tilby points out, this is a key principle within the Anglican tradition, and an area where she perceives a difficulty in some fresh expressions of Church:

> Until quite recently we have always been able to say that if you want to know what Anglicans *believe*, take part in our

liturgical worship. I am not sure that all fresh expressions initiatives would permit that discernment to be made. (Croft, 2008, p. 82)

The writings that have flowed from the Second Vatican Council have influenced the ecclesial lives of many who are not members of the Roman Catholic Church. However, the issues raised by fresh expressions, their foundation and their relationship to the wider Church are only just beginning to be explored in this context. It is to be hoped that there will emerge more fresh expressions that find secure ecclesial roots and a cogent understanding of the sacramental nature of the Church, so as to ensure a balance of paradigms within emerging expressions of Church. A renewed emphasis upon the sacramental (and specifically eucharistic) nature of the Church is essential if it is to be true to itself and its calling, and also to proclaim the fullness of the gospel and the kingdom. We have too easily relegated such ontological truths into a murky and uneasy background, rather than seeing them as essential and integral to the ways of living of the kingdom.

Initial criticisms of the concept of fresh expressions from an ecclesiological perspective can only assist the same in becoming what they are intended to be. By the same token, a rigorous application of a model that embraces the totality of that mission, with a keen priority given to issues of social justice, can only benefit the task. Fresh expressions of Church do not drop down, fully formed, from the sky. In common with the life of the whole Church, they are in the process of becoming, and it will be through the stories and emerging praxis of fresh expressions that criticisms are either answered or ignored.

Prayerful attention, strategic thinking and robust action in the sphere of local, national and global social justice issues may bring about two specific advantages to fresh expressions of Church within the mixed economy. First, because they are participating in what is right and true, they will draw closer to God's image for them, and therefore closer to God. Second, fidelity to social justice concerns means that a more balanced understanding of mission results, redressing the balance away from what for many is a consumerist tendency within the Church to see mission as merely a numerical exercise. Wherever the Church seeks justification by numerical size and advance alone, there is collusion with the unhealthy acquisitive habits of a society so frequently criticized by the Church for this very tendency.

The unchurched will not trust a church that preaches one thing and does another. In an age and a culture where profit is privatized for the few, while debt is socialized as a burden for the many, we need forms of Church that are prepared to assert again and again the intrinsic and holy worthiness of the individual alongside the need for genuine common good – forms that speak and act against greed and half-truth within political decision-making processes, for the good not merely of its members, but for all.

> To love someone is to desire that person's good and to take effective steps to secure it. Besides the good of the individual, there is a good that is linked to living in society: the common good. It is the good of 'all of us', made up of individuals, families and intermediate groups who together constitute society. It is a good that is sought not only for its own sake, but also for the people who belong to the social community and who can only really and effectively pursue their good within it. To desire the *common good* and strive towards it is a requirement of *justice* and *charity*. (Benedict XVI, 2009, para. 7)

Will the fresh expressions movement, encouraged by bishops and church leaders, seek as a priority to promote forms of Church that see this work of advocacy as central to the work of alleviating poverty? This would mean not merely the 'detached' advocacy of diocesan boards and officers, but also the local and direct means of building up those who have been knocked down, as focused fresh expressions projects work in partnership with other local agencies to promote a heightened sense of individual and community esteem.

This is true about local issues as much as national ones.

Given a mixed economy in which the *source* of fresh expressions is itself mixed, both from parishes and network churches, a fresh expression is as likely – at least for now – to be dealing in the same sort of issues that might affect a local parish community. So a fresh expression for young people in a village, intent on pressing for better facilities for young people, might well be campaigning for the same thing, regardless of its source – parish or network. Given the nature of some (though by no means all) fresh expressions to operate in networks that can appear to be very much like interest groups, will this lead to a more self-interested approach, to the exclusion of the wider picture to which Hull alludes? Only time will tell. It is both interesting and instructive to reflect upon the life and mission of the Corrymeela Community in this regard. Formed some 45 years ago in response to the deep-seated social and civil unrest in Northern Ireland, its work of reconciliation in that land and beyond has become a byword for a ministry that has assisted in profound transformation. It is presently sustained by a praying community, in diaspora, of over 150 members and 5,000 friends, operating very much as a network. Portraying the hallmarks of a way of being that mirrors more recent new-monasticism, the Corrymeela Community should be of special interest to the fresh expressions movement. It is an example of what might be achieved in response to a specific local need. It combines the best of residential and dispersed community. It is sustained, self-evidently, by intercessory prayer and communications over a global network. It is, perhaps, an example for the contemporary fresh expressions leadership of what a mature fresh expression, formed in the power of the Spirit and in response to specific social and political issues, might become in the fullness of time.

The political era in which we live has modelled the notion of a 'Big Society', with characteristics such as decentralization, volunteering, support for new social enterprises and the publication of information to empower local communities. (see report, 'Building the Big Society') It is into such a context that the Church moves. The critical necessity for the Church in any form to be active in community involvement and social justice is as strong as ever. Rowan Williams (2010) sees the shape of the Church offering a positive model for this concept:

And the Church has got to model for the world a participatory, active, sometimes argumentative interaction between its own elements, so that society understands that it is not a monolithic block, nor a fiction which simply cloaks a mass of unrelated individuals, but yes, a community of communities.

Perhaps this notion is further enhanced by one of the strongest images in Pope Benedict's theology – that of the Church as family.[11] This holds at several levels – the familial relationships conferred at baptism, the deep relationships formed within the local church community, the relationship of churches within a diocese, and so forth. It is an *intimate* image both for the mixed economy church and for the task of emerging churches.

Conclusions

Given the diverse nature of fresh expressions, and the type of theological questioning that has emerged thus far, it seems pertinent to end not with safe conclusions, but rather with a series of pleas. The first plea is for a return for what we might consider to be the root of fresh expressions thinking – that of the intuitive approach to mission, and hence the complex business of discernment – 'finding out what God is doing, and joining in'.[12] That is a process which is far too whimsically applied in a good deal of fresh expressions thinking. Discernment is the task of the whole Church, not simply a local enclave of it. It is a task that places the Church at the service of God's will, and therefore has no agenda that is not Christ's. We have sat too lightly to the classic hermeneutical processes. Perhaps a reappraisal of the *purpose* of fresh expressions is needed, illustrating not merely the desire to proclaim a 'growing' Church but to engage more thoroughly with core mission values. Critical engagement with the principles of social justice and kingdom theology can only assist that endeavour.

Second, the issue of the foundation of fresh expressions

needs to be addressed. One of the most attractive features of this initiative was that new communities were to be formed in response to something – namely, a discernment process in which, guided by the Holy Spirit, the Church would act in response to a given situation – a need, a prompting, an as yet unserved community of people. Too often pressure from more central structures to form fresh expressions, especially in diocesan mission strategies, can lead to an inspiration that is other than that of the Holy Spirit.

The third plea is for a renewed and renewing emphasis upon issues of social justice, the dignity of the individual, the adoption of local and global issues, as specific tasks for the fresh expressions movement. New church communities should provide opportunities for people of vision to engage directly with issues of concern and to set up appropriate networks for dialogue. This is particularly the case when a group emerges in response to a specific concern. To have a human issue (homelessness, drug misuse, family support) as the prior impulse for the forming of a church community is a strong hand indeed. The discernment required to guide this in such a way that it is neither stifled nor stifling, but rather enhanced with a yet fuller expression of Church, is a tremendous challenge for pioneer leaders and those charged with training them and caring for them.

This leads to a reminder that fresh expressions, whatever their perceived faults and failings, are (with venerable exceptions like Corrymeela) very young indeed, and will take time to find their true place within the wider economy of the Church. My fourth plea is therefore for a great deal of patience – something the Church needs to learn again and to teach in its turn.

The present age has seen a considerable change and deterioration in the perception of faith, people of faith and their leaders. Scandals, arguments and acts of terror, with religious labels variously attached, have provided no little impetus for that deterioration. Perhaps part of the gift of fresh expressions of Church at this time might be that a page of this particular book is turned, as our service to God and neighbour is renewed in grace and faith, and as the Church learns again from those who are new to the faith, and remembers again the call 'to animate temporal realities with Christian commitment, by which [they] show that they are witnesses and agents of peace and justice' (John Paul II, 1987, 47 # 6; cf. 42).

References

Anglican Church Communion, 1984, *Bonds of Affection*; 1990, *Mission in a Broken World*, online at: http://www.anglican communion. org/ministry/mission/fivemarks.cfm [Accessed 2 January 2011]

Archbishops' Council, 2004, *Mission-shaped Church*, London: Church House Publishing

Archbishops' Council, 1994, *Breaking New Ground*, London: Church House Publishing

Graham Cray, 2010, 'We are all "for the parish"', online at: http:// www.freshexpressions.org.uk/news/cen/201011parish [Accessed 2 January 2011]

Stephen Croft, 2008, *Mission-shaped Questions*, London: Church House Publishing

Benedict XVI, 2006, *Caritas in Veritate*, online at: http://www.vatican. va/holy_father/benedict_xvi/encyclicals/documents/hf_ben-xvi_enc_ 20090629_caritas-in-veritate_en.html [Accessed 16 March 2012]

Benedict XVI, 2009, *Deus Caritas Est*, online at: http://www.vatican. va/holy_father/benedict_xvi/encyclicals/documents/hf_ben-xvi_ enc_20051225_deus-caritas-est_en.html [Accessed 20 March 2012]

Andrew Davison and Alison Milbank, 2010, *For the Parish*, London: SCM Press

Avery Dulles, 2009, *Evangelization for the Third Millennium*, Mahwah, NJ: Paulist Press

Austin Farrer, 1952, *The Crown of the Year*, London: Dacre Press

Government report, 2010, 'Building the Big Society', Cabinet Office, online at http://www.cabinetoffice.gov.uk/sites/default/files/resources/ building-big-society_0.pdf [Accessed 2 October 2011]

S. W. Hahn, 2009, *Covenant and Communion*, London: Darton, Longman & Todd

Stanley Hauerwas and Samuel Wells, 2004, *Blackwell Companion to Christian Ethics*, London: Blackwell

John Hull, 2006, *Mission-shaped Church: A Theological Response*, London: SCM Press

George Lings, 2003, 'Mass Planting', in *Encounters on the Edge* (16), Church Army

Donald McGavran, 1955, *The Bridges of God*, London: World Dominion Press

John Paul II, 1987, *Sollicitudo Rei Socialis* (47 # 6; cf. 42), online at: http://www.vatican.va/holy_father/john_paul_ii/encyclicals/documents/ hf_jp-ii_enc_30121987_sollicitudo-rei-socialis_en.html [Accessed on 16 March 2012]

Lesslie Newbigin, 1989, *The Gospel in a Pluralist Society*, Grand Rapids: Eerdmans

Joseph Ratzinger, 1987, *Principles of Catholic Theology*, San Francisco: Ignatius Press

Rowan Williams, 2010, 'How Should Churches Respond to the Big Society?', online at: http://www.archbishopofcanterbury.org/articles. php/571/how-should-churches-respond-to-the-big-society-rowan- williams [Accessed 16 March 2012]

Appendix: List of encyclical and other documents

Rerum Novarum (On the condition of labour), Leo XIII, 1891

Quadragesimo Annus (After Forty Years), Pius XI, 1931

Mater et Magistra (Christianity and Social Progress), John XXIII, 1961

Pacem in Terris (Peace on Earth), John XXIII, 1963

Gaudium et Spes (Pastoral Constitution on the Church in the Modern World), Vatican II, 1965

Populorum Progressio (On the development of peoples), Paul VI, 1967

Octagesima Adveniens (A call to action), Paul VI, 1971

Justicia in Mundo (Justice in the World), Synod of Bishops, 1971

Laborem Exercens (On Human Work), John Paul II, 1981

Solicitudo Rei Socialis (On Social Concern), John Paul II, 1987

Centesimus Annus (The Hundredth Year), John Paul II, 1991

Evangelium Vitae (The Gospel of Life), John Paul II, 1995

Fidis et Ratio (Faith and Reason), John Paul II, 1998

Deus Caritas Est (God is love), Benedict XVI, 2005

Saramentum Caritatis (Apostolic Exhortation on the Eucharist), Benedict XVI, 2007

Caritas in Veritate (In Charity and Truth), Benedict XVI, 2009

Notes

1 See for example http://www.emergingchurch.info/reflection/rowan williams/index.htm [Accessed 2 January 2011].

2 All these encyclicals are available from the following website for the Office for Social Justice for St. Paul and Minneapolis. This is also the website that summarizes the 'Ten Principles' of the 16 major documents in question. I am grateful to Kathleen Tomlin, Director for the St. Paul and Minneapolis Catholic Office for Social Justice, for her support, and for the excellent summary and resources offered for this subject.

DAMIAN FEENEY

The encyclical titles can be found in the above Appendix. Online at:
http://www.osjspm.org/page.aspx?pid=436 [Accessed 2 January 2011].

3 For more information, see http://www.osjspm.org/page.aspx?
pid=436 [Accessed 16 March 2012].

4 It should be recognized, here and elsewhere, that there is a distinction made between *evangelism* and *evangelization* (the preferred term for Catholic authors such as Dulles). It may be helpful to quote Dulles himself:

> Many Christians … grant the importance of evangelization in theory but shy away from it in practice. Very often … they have a narrow and inadequate conception of the term. Perhaps they are put off by certain styles of evangelism … often it settles for merely verbal or emotional responses in which people profess an experience of Christ as their personal Saviour. In sharp contrast to this narrow concept, Catholicism looks upon evangelization as a complex process consisting of many elements. Among these elements, wrote Pope Paul VI, are 'the renewal of humanity, witness, explicit proclamation, inner adherence, entry into the community, acceptance of signs, apostolic initiative'. (2009, p. 3)

I suspect this is a model which many Anglicans today would label as 'evangelism'.

5 Bishop Graham Cray's full response to Davison and Milbank can be found here: [Online] http://www.freshexpressions.org.uk/news/cen/201011parish [Accessed 2 January 2011].

6 For more information, see http://www.leadingyourchurchinto growth.org.uk [Accessed 16 March 2012].

7 I am grateful to Canon Robin Gamble for this particular term.

8 I am grateful to George Lings for this analogy, first used with regard to the Church congregation planted in an ASDA Supermarket in Preston. See 'Mass Planting', 2003, *Encounters on the Edge* (16), Church Army.

9 See Davison and Milbank, 2010, p. 65.

10 Attributed to Prosper of Aquitaine (*c.* 435–42 CE) by Nicholas A. Jesson, online at: http://ecumenism.net/archive/jesson_lexorandi.pdf [Accessed on 2 January 2011].

11 For example see p. 128 of Hahn, 2009.

12 See the following webpage for example: http://www.archbishop-ofcanterbury.org/976 [Accessed on 2 January 2011].

13

Paradise in Peckham: Signs of the Kingdom

TOBY WRIGHT

The radical, committed to human liberation, does not become the prisoner of a 'circle of certainty' within which reality is also imprisoned. On the contrary, the more radical the person is, the more fully he or she enters into reality so that, knowing it better, he or she can better transform it. (Freire, 1993, p. 21)

As a parish priest in Peckham, I had the immense privilege to serve for five years in an area that possessed people of immense faith and friendliness. My vocation led me from leafy Petersfield into the heart of urban Peckham, where I was fortunate to be able to enter into the reality of lives seeking transformation in the midst of the many challenges. At the extreme end of these challenges lay the well-publicized tragedy of violence and gangs.

The church in Peckham was under the patronage of John Chrysostom, a saint born in Antioch around the year 349 CE. It seemed extraordinary that this man who had been so instrumental in the lives of Christians in Antioch and Constantinople should be watching over us in Peckham at the start of a new millennium. Aideen Hartley, in his book *John Chrysostom and the Transformation of the City*, wrote that Chrysostom 'is concerned about the distractions posed by an increasingly worldly city, and by a perceived breakdown in order and morality' (p. 9). Chrysostom was further concerned that in his urban ministry there was a danger that the signs of the kingdom would become so hidden, that the members of his flock would simply fade into the background of the ancient city.

In one of the most poignant chapters of my ministry, I went to a young man's birthday party. I had seen him recently as his uncle had just died traumatically from cancer a few weeks before. When I arrived there was a banner on the front door reading, 'Its time to party'. Only it wasn't.

This young man had been murdered two weeks earlier, stabbed to death by another young man on the streets of South London. He had bled to death in the arms of a friend. His friend had cradled him, like an image of the pieta. When the emergency services tried to take the young man's body, the friend couldn't bring himself to let go.

In ministering to the family and friends of this young man, I was brought face to face with the power of God's Kingdom to reach even the darkest places. It brought a renewed sense of how the structure and form of ancient Christian practices continue to speak powerfully in our day to those who are spiritually searching.

Sadly such stories are not isolated, and the Christian communities across our cities and towns have the distressing task of ministering to those whose lives have been turned upside down and irrevocably shaken by the tragedy of violence. There are some extraordinary stories of individuals and organizations who are called by God to minister to those who are on the edge of violence, those seeking to escape from life in gangs, or those whose loved ones have been killed through gun and knife crime. An important contribution to this is *Fighting Chance: Tackling Britain's Gang Culture*, by Patrick Regan.

Such realities challenge us in what can so often be the relative comfort of our Christian faith. What is the kingdom all about? The kingdom is the life in which we are called out of our routines. A calling that reminds us that all that is created will be called back into the Kingdom of Christ. A calling that will lead to this world being turned upside down in order to establish a reign of compassion and caring, healing and flourishing. This is what it means when we pray, 'thy kingdom come'.

In a culture that treasures the individual, the kingdom calls us to a communal life. In a culture that treasures spontaneity, the kingdom calls us to something enduring. In a culture that suggests that truth is a construct of the mind, the kingdom calls us to experience truth in mind and body. In a culture that treasures relevance, the kingdom calls us to a deeper relevance the world does not yet know.

As part of the response to entering the reality, as Freire puts it, a small group of priests began to develop Glorious. This was the fragile beginning of an urban fresh expression that recognized sacraments as evangelistic tools and enabled the young people within our communities to engage with the Church from wherever they happen to be. Young people from various churches were involved in the process of making the audiovisual material through workshops, and they contributed throughout the liturgy in drama, music and a ministry of welcome. The idea for Glorious developed out of the ministry of Blessed in Portsmouth diocese, and grew a new identity in the predominantly Afro-Caribbean context of the Old Kent Road.

There are many more advanced fresh expressions and often these have a far greater emphasis on developing new communities of faith than we managed to form. However, for us it was an adventure into something contextual and new that spoke in culturally relevant ways to some of the young people in an urban environment. The signs of the kingdom were around us and among us as we looked at the context with fresh vision.

The paradise that is promised by Christ was made present in the signs of broken bread and wine poured out for us in love. In a context where order and morality are often perceived to be breaking down, God's Kingdom was seen to be constantly breaking in; into lives of suffering and pain, the kingdom is leading Christian communities to break out of circles of certainty and to embrace the true reality of kingdom life. A life, as C. S. Lewis put it, that is 'dazzling, radiant ... pulsating all through with ... energy, joy and wisdom and love as we cannot now imagine'. It is these signs of the kingdom that are true signs of hope. It is the reality of these signs of the kingdom that means that here and now we see paradise in Peckham.

References

Paulo Freire, 1993, *Pedagogy of the Oppressed*, London: Penguin

Aideen Hartley, 2004, *John Chrysostom and the Transformation of the City*, London: Duckworth

Patrick Regan, 2010, *Fighting Chance*, London: Hodder & Stoughton

14

Addicted in the City

CLARE CATFORD

Huddled under a soggy cardboard box in a city subway, in freezing temperatures, a twenty-something homeless man begs for cash; it's not for a sandwich. It's the end of a classy dinner party in one of London's leafier suburbs, and the designer food has come and gone; now it's the turn of the designer drugs. It's 10 a.m., and a harassed mum has had enough of changing nappies and appeasing her two angry toddlers under five, and downs a large swig of vodka, neat. A student at one of the country's top universities can't stand the way she looks and feels inside. She gorges three bars of chocolate, four packets of crisps and two slices of thick white bread with peanut butter loaded on top, in three minutes flat. She then throws the lot up in the loo, hoping that her flatmates won't hear her retching.

Addiction knows no boundaries. Heroin users can be found wandering the city streets, in top banking institutions and at fashionable book launches. Ecstasy's cheap and cheerful appeal means it's a clubber's favourite. 'Why not? It's been a hard day hairdressing/plumbing/banking/managing/reporting/ diagnosing.' The judge who downs two large whiskies before a demanding trial begins is just as much of an addict as the bored and wealthy shopper who cannot stop spending at his shiny new shopping centre. Priests, politicians and police officers are all vulnerable.

According to recent statistics, one in three of us struggle with substance addiction and millions more suffer from addiction to work or sex or other behaviours. There are many theories as to why one person is an addict and another is not.[1] Experts have debated whether there is a genetic component to addictive behaviour; others claim environmental factors are more influential. After working with addicts for many years, the counsellor, theologian and author John Bradshaw suggests that 'the drivenness in any addiction is about the ruptured self, the belief that one is flawed as a person. The content of the addiction, whether it is alcoholism or work, is an attempt at an intimate relationship. The workaholic with her work or the alcoholic with his booze are having a love affair. Each one mood-alters to avoid the feeling of loneliness and hurt in the underbelly of shame' (1988, p. 67; Catford, 2008).

The stigma that attaches itself to those who are stuck in this compulsive behaviour pattern adds to the shame and feelings of hopelessness. Addiction is often hidden, reinforcing the sufferer's sense of isolation and powerlessness. 'It is hard not to blame a man who is drinking himself to death. Or a woman whose baby is born addicted to heroin. But what are we blaming them for? For being weak or selfish or stupid? Just like the rest of us?' (RCP, 2004, p. 1). The repetitive cycles of bingeing and purging, behaviours familiar to the anorexic and bulimic, will also seem bizarre and disgusting to those who will not, or cannot understand them. But of course there are many reasons why these actions can be so compelling for those who subscribe to them: they fulfil a need, a yearning and, most profoundly, they can be an expression of deep childhood wounding. 'Anorexic women shut out nurturance for fear that it will somehow poison them: "People being close to me makes me sick. Food makes me sick. The distance I keep from people and food, makes me feel pure ... and ... safer". The metaphor for bulimia is accepting nurturance, and, finding it poisonous, casting it out' (Davis Kasl, 1990, p. 184).

If these compulsions are 'blemishes of individual character, perceived as weak will ... and ... unnatural passions ... inferred from a known record of ... addiction (and) alcoholism', then of course those who suffer from such afflictions will inevitably be subject to discrimination (Goffman, 1990, pp. 14–15). However, because addiction is so common, perhaps it is a way of communicating; it is a language with its own vocabulary; a scream for the recognition of past pain and alienation.

This alienation is part and parcel of living in a busy city environment. In work or out of it, rich or poor, esteemed or ignored, addictions are a coping strategy. They are a way of filling the hole in the soul, rebelling against a materialistic message and mindset that shouts 'more is better'; and a way of blocking that voice that sits on our shoulders and tells us we are 'not good enough, not rich enough, not loving enough, not holy enough and not acceptable enough'.

Addictions are powerful and isolating. Online forums often provide a sense of community for sufferers, where there is none to speak of in a real human context. This is an excerpt from 'Steve's Story' on an internet mental health forum:

> I am currently diagnosed as Bi-polar Disorder with secondary depression and cannabis dependency (although the BPD diagnosis is currently under review as the waters have been muddied with my cannabis use). What was previously contained as words in my head as opposed to physical emotions, have now become quite crippling to the point where I would consider myself more ill now than I have been in about 3 years'. ('Steve', members only discussion forum)[2]

The bi-polar diagnosis together with the addictive struggle is a complex challenge for families, relatives, friends and health practitioners. Clearly addiction is widespread among those struggling with their mental health: 'In the UK it is estimated that one-third of psychiatric patients with serious mental illness have a substance misuse problem' (RCP, 2003, p. 2).

Alcoholism, drug addiction, eating disorders and sex addiction (this list is not exhaustive) are behaviours that provide temporary comfort from perceived or real pain. One interpretation goes further than this. 'Part of the tremendous power of addictions is that they offer ways of avoiding the threat of non-being. Addictions are ... desperate strategies by which we attempt to avoid the unimaginable terror of non-existence' (Firman and Gila, 1997, p. 15).

Gerri is a sex addict. She uses sex to fill 'that empty place inside' (Davis Kasl, 1990, p. 75). She describes her descent into despair: 'nothing worked any more ... I was always sneaking around, lying, and feeling paranoid that one of the four guys I was seeing would bump into one another and there would be a great scene' (Davis Kasl, p. 73). The more her shame was triggered, the worse the addiction became. She contemplated suicide before she found a 12-step programme (a spiritual path for addicts) designed to help those who compulsively seek a sexual high. It is common for addicts who suffer from chronic shame and/or depression to have been born into families that have similar traits; and/or to have been abused sexually and emotionally themselves. 'I found porn underneath my dad's bed when I was 7. I felt better when I looked at it; although I also felt it was wrong. I know my dad had other women. My mum turned a blind eye' (a 'share' at a 12-step Sex Addicts recovery group, June 2010, London). Patterns of behaviour can be set up from then on, and an addictive high can boost the feel-good chemicals that reduce the anxiety that a corti-sol-flooded brain (called the 'stress' hormone) experiences. These patterns need to be broken in order to heal: 'part of the recovery process is learning to be gentle; to accept yourself – obsessions, mistakes, imperfections, addictions ... to stop shaming yourself or being ashamed of your shame' (Davis Kasl, 1990, p. 282).

Addictive behaviour is simply one way that shame and unresolved pain can manifest. As one alcoholic and depression sufferer expresses it, 'by the time I tried to kill myself, it was because I had lost all hope of pulling out of it' (Brampton, 2008, p. 242). Love and acceptance from a Christian or spiritual community can have a significant influence. This requires a response that is inclusive and affirming. 'A starting place for Christian community is the dispelling of the myth that pain and suffering have nothing to do with the human journey of becoming ... knowing that we are cared for, and that our carers suffer similarly, makes our pain somehow more bearable' (Mobsby, 2008, p. 127). Wherever the complete person is accepted, with their addictions and the subsequent shame that emerges, this is, in itself, a manifestation of love – which those subscribing to a religious tradition might interpret as God's love.

When someone suffers from addiction, mental illness, and disabling shame, 'Why me?' is a common question; the need to reflect on 'why' suffering occurs seems to be a perennial human concern. As Paul Lanham, a London priest who suffers from depression, expresses it: 'there is so much anguish that seems random ... the ancient idea of God sitting on a cloud arbitrarily throwing thunderbolts at people ... they hit some and miss others. People who are depressed may apply this notion directly to themselves' (Lanham, 2005, p. 13). 'For years I felt so bad that I blamed no-one but myself. I internalized all the anger, the blame my abuser dumped on me. This led to a deep depression' (Desmond, 2004, p. 19). This depression sufferer identifies with the Psalmist who describes his own despair, and cries out to God: 'You have put me in the lowest pit, in the darkest depths, your wrath lies heavily upon me; you have overwhelmed me with all your waves' (Ps. 88.6–7). This expression of despair also manifests a longing for some kind of resolution and relationship; a longing for the pain to be acknowledged and heard.

In a sense, this cry to the God of his understanding shows that religious belief can be instrumental in expressing pain, shame and despair; an excruciating dialogue between the human and the divine. Others, who may not subscribe to a particular belief system, or have been shamed and damaged by it, may feel that they do not find biblical or religious language useful. It is worth acknowledging too, that even those with religious belief can come to the conclusion that God is absent, that no one cares, and that they are completely alone – the experience of depression and shame being so alienating from the self, the community and any kind of spirituality. It is as if this wounding is so deep and the alienation so profound, that death or non-existence can feel as if it is just around the corner, prompting so great a terror it can be inconceivable to imagine a way out of the abyss.

If shame and depression are in part 'a wounding to the spirit', then the converse is also true. (Firman and Gila, 1997,

p. 66). 'The blossoming of the human spirit seems to imply an intimate union between body and soul' (Firman and Gila, pp. 67–8).

Clearly there is not one consenting view of how spirituality, be it religious or otherwise, can be expressed. The pastoral theologian, Clinebell, outlines four basic spiritual needs: '[the need] for a meaningful philosophy of life, and a challenging object of self-investment, for a sense of the numinous and transcendent, for deep experience of trustful relatedness to God, other people, and nature [and to] fulfil the "image of God" within oneself by developing one's truest humanity through creativity, awareness and inward freedom' (Clinebell, 2000, p. 94).

Getting to grips with the pain of shame and depression in a community that provides a spiritual programme with honesty, forgiveness of self and others, and making amends where appropriate, are some of the aims of many 12-step recovery groups. Just one of the promises that's read out at the start of every such group goes: 'We begin to accept our imperfections and mistakes as part of being human, healing our shame and perfectionism while working on our character defects.'[3] Sex and Love Addicts Anonymous, for example, welcomes anyone who struggles with dysfunctional attachment, obsessions, sexual acting out and sexual anorexia (the terror of having intimate relationships at all). It takes great courage to break through the denial of addiction and acknowledge the need for help and support from a spiritual community.

Sex and Love Addicts Anonymous is just one of many addiction recovery fellowships based on the Alcoholics Anonymous 12-step model. AA formed in the United States in the 1930s. It emerged from the Oxford Group movement, a Christian organization, which was the major founder of the 12-step AA programme, the umbrella organization from which all subsequent anonymous fellowships emerged.

Over the years the steps were fine-tuned so that those who had little or no faith could join as long as they were prepared to surrender their will to a 'power greater than themselves'. 'Faith in a Power greater than ourselves, and miraculous demonstrations of that power in human lives, are facts as old as man himself' (Bill W., 1939, p. 55). The steps encourage self-acceptance, as well as acceptance of a higher power, however the addict defines that. This acceptance has a theological foundation. 'The psychotherapeutic injunction that the basis for acceptance for others is self-acceptance has its deeper ontological root in the Christian proclamation that the basis for the freedom to love the neighbour is the forgiveness of God' (Tillich, 2002, p. 5).

Community is also an essential part of this kind of spiritual, physical and emotional recovery. 'In the beauty and fragility of this experience [of community] lies also its pain. [It] provides the necessary safeguards and limits but also the support to allow us to live fully these experiences of joy and pain' (Vanier, 1988, pp. 94–6). The 12-step experience is by no means perfect; it is made up of human beings, who clearly are not. But bizarrely it is in the acceptance of our own and others' imperfections that freedom emerges. 'We find a common denominator in our obsessive/compulsive patterns which renders any personal differences of sexual or gender orientation irrelevant.'[4]

Spirituality, as indicated, is not experienced in isolation. If we take the perspective that '[spirituality] is our ability to be in relationship with God, our seeking after a religious answer to the question of existence … our ability to develop, to actualize the spiritual dimension of our lives, depends upon the meeting of our other needs'; trust, or even faith in the other can be the bedrock from which a healthy and nurturing spirituality flourishes (Kammer, 1988, p. 100). If our primary carers were unable to meet our psychological, emotional and spiritual needs as children, we experience not only a psychological, physical and emotional betrayal, but a spiritual abandonment too. 'If these persons were not trustworthy, if they provided erratic care, often responded with neglect or cruelty, it may never be possible for us to trust the fundamental goodness of existence' (Kammer, p. 101). Thus the choices we make, particularly in the realm of relationships, can be compulsive and addictive, prompting attachments that may be abusive and harmful to all aspects of ourselves, including our spiritual development.

If abuse is our childhood pattern, then there can be a tendency to choose relationships that simply reinforce the blueprint of connections that are painful and familiar. 'Many people suffer terrible relationships ... they give themselves away, piece by piece. They will accept ... exploitative (and violent) relationships, an addicted and repeatedly unfaithful spouse, the second-class status of mistress' – the list can be a long one (Carnes, 1997, p. 204). The city can be a lonely place. Sometimes any relationship, no matter how harmful or painful, can feel better than no relationship at all. Even if we are experiencing abuse, then at least we are alive.

'For those who fear abandonment because of childhood wounding the shift to a positive regard for oneself, and a desire for time with oneself is one of the key developmental changes that an abusive environment may have blocked' (Carnes). The desire for connectedness with 'the other' is a human drive. 'Striving for connectedness, for relatedness, in Christian terms, for reconciliation ... is one of our most profound human needs' (Carnes). Inevitably, a dysfunctional and abusive relationship is a distortion of this desire, and will reinforce our shame further, never providing the connectedness we crave.

The spiritual fallout from abuse is devastating. As one survivor expresses it, 'I lose myself; I am re-living what my parents did to me, over and over. I cry to some kind of God. I don't know if I can leave this man, he hurts me all the time, I want to leave him, but I don't want to be alone; I am frightened of him hurting me if I do. Sometimes I feel suicidal (*she weeps*).'[5] If the abused begins a spiritual journey – in a 12-step fellowship, with a spiritual director, and/or a therapist who is attuned to the need for the transcendent – then there can be change, sometimes as profound as a metaphorical resurrection from a living death. Paul Lanham's acceptance of his long-term depression was, in a sense, his liberation. 'We do not have to deserve love, or to feel loved in order to be loved; we are loved for ourselves ... this is the doctrine of grace ... which lies near the doctrine of the Cross' (Lanham, 2005, p. 16).

Patrick Carnes is the clinical director for sexual disorders at The Meadows, a recovery and rehabilitation centre in Arizona. He helps his clients, who are often in despair about their lives and in great shame and pain, to recognize spirituality in a number of ways. 'Crisis and pain force surrender, accepting the realities we have tried to flee, when we accept suffering, we reconnect with the deeper rhythms of the universe, never again will we let things not matter. We are part of a larger purpose' (Carnes, 1997, 2005).

His thoughts are echoed by the theologian Henri Nouwen, who describes three essential characteristics of the spiritual life. '[Firstly] the connection with the self and the acceptance of your own brokenness, [next] the acceptance of the community and a renewed trust in others; [and] the ability to trust oneself and others clears the path to trusting a creator' (1975, p. 1).

What has all this got to do with mission and fresh expressions of Church? Well, first, 12-step fellowships have a lot to teach the local church. I believe these are remarkable places of encounter with God, where people come together in their brokenness to share their pain in a profound and hopeful expression of the human need for redemptive communion, with others and with God, in which healing is found, and where life-giving support is provided. Fresh expressions would do well to reflect on the 12-step approach as they discern the vocation to form ecclesial communities out of contextual mission. Church can sometimes feel essentially judgemental and not easy to belong to. 12-step groups embody concrete acceptance, and a deeply practical form of pastoral care that can help people to experience and encounter God from within their own experiences. As a member of a 12-step group, one is not required to be anything other than what one is; God, or my friend, meets me where I am. An encounter with God in the midst of one's experiences, of one's brokenness, is surely at the heart of the gospel message. If this depth of acceptance were a stable feature of the mission of fresh expressions of Church, they would truly be visible manifestations of the invisible Kingdom of God. I have experienced something of this acceptance in the Moot Community, my spiritual home for some years now. We remember that in the New Testament the most common word for Church is the Greek word 'ecclesia', which from the beginning included slaves, women, children and all those who were marginalized under the power of the Roman Empire – including, no doubt, addicts of all kinds. The Church is, then and now, a visible yet incomplete expression of divine acceptance, which brings healing through belonging as it lives out God's love-mission to the world.

Some have developed discipleship courses using elements of the 12-step programme.[6] In fact the Moot Community used the first three steps as the basis for a Lent course orientated around the mission needs of those who were spiritual seekers and curious about the Christian faith. The content then centred on knowing that you cannot fix yourself, that there is a God who loves you and seeks your fulfilment, which can be discovered only by letting go, or surrendering. So many today have some form of addiction, so it made perfect sense to combine Lent as a season of exploration with the structure of a 12-step group.

Authentic Christian spirituality – a spirituality that involves humility, a determination to be honest with ourselves, with others and the God of our understanding – can be key to recovery from suffering. 'People relentlessly attempt to calm their inner turbulence ... their pain and suffering ... by all manner of therapy and (hollow) spirituality. They seek refuge (and spend a great deal of money) on each new programme or method as if it involved a final resolution' (O'Donohue, 1998, p. 215). In a sense this is completely logical. Sometimes the pain of shame and depression can be so overwhelming – grabbing at straws and trying to get a short-term fix can seem better than endless nothingness, self-hate and emotional impotence.

This is the challenge facing Christian communities today. It is real, frightening and messy. If these communities are not aware of their own shadows, then they will not tolerate the shadows of others whose vulnerabilities consciously or unconsciously remind them of their own human frailties. Stephen Pattison emphasizes that there is a cost to many religious communities when they begin to address shame and its frequent partner, depression. '[Religious communities must] turn from an idealizing dualism. This is an enormous price to pay in terms of fundamental identity, thought and practice' (Pattison, 2000, p. 286).

I have heard it said in some churches that pain and suffering are an outrage, an aberration and evidence of our own sin. Addiction reminds us that suffering, to the contrary, is part of the human condition, and pain goes hand in hand with life and the challenge of faith to grow into all maturity – where all of us are called to face our hurts, and grow. Those who suffer with addiction know about sin; they need to hear far more about love and hope, something the Church is not always good at showing and expressing. The mission of fresh expressions must be born out of an awareness, at the heart of each community, of our own shadow, and be motivated by a desire to share the joyful discovery of God's saving love.

To question our own idealized God, both individually and collectively, needs courage and a desire for authenticity, which inevitably will mean individual and collective pain. Perhaps there is a need to 'unlearn' a particular view of the Godself, which we have gripped on to like a liferaft because we fear an unknown alternative. Perhaps there is the terror of being excluded from a much-loved group, because we dare to re-evaluate our faith in the light of the darkness and messiness of our own existence or that of someone we hold dear. These are daunting steps for even the most mature religious individual or community to take; and it is understandable, though regrettable, that many will not or cannot journey down the 'road less travelled' (Peck, 1987).

Human beings do not naturally choose a path of pain. Who would actively seek to embrace this kind of mental, physical and spiritual crucifixion? As Alison observes, 'The person who is put in the place of "being cursed" feels all the pain and shame of ostracism. Any one of us would do anything we could to avoid such a fate' (2006, p. 204). The link with Christ here is obvious. Perhaps, as Alison suggests, Jesus went 'voluntarily into that space ... designated as "cursed by God" ... and occupied it peacefully ... and he was seen by his disciples as having occupied that space ... Coming among them still peacefully ... they could pass this onto others' (Alison, p. 205). Christ was the scapegoat. He bore the brunt of all the projected fear and anger that his enemies could not face in themselves; a parallel with all the pain a shamed or depressed person may feel has been or is directed at them. How to tolerate a person who, by just being, exposes our own darkness? Murder him, ostracize and ridicule him. Then those of us who feel we belong to the 'normals' can continue to bolster our own fragile self-esteem by holding those who suffer in contempt, and continue to shame those who trigger our own vulnerabilities.

One woman describes her journey thus: 'God has become my everything. I know that without my faith I would not have survived the child sexual abuse ... the abusive relationships ... the suicide attempts by my son, the loneliness and abandonment of my partners and the church ... I could go on and on. My faith allows me to try and forgive, forget and move on ... the pain is always there. I do have the hope of my faith, and that is all that matters' (Loewenthal, 2007, p. 135). It is often self-forgiveness, however, that is the biggest challenge. The phrase, 'forgive us our sins' in the Lord's Prayer might be interpreted in part as 'forgive us when we have valued ourselves too little' – a sin of omission.

We live in a broken world. Our parents or carers may have done us great wrongs; we may have been subjected to ridicule from the society we inhabit; we may have been or continue to be ostracized by a religious community and we may have been victim of appalling tragedy and conflict with the legacy of a wound that may never heal. We may simply have had the misfortune to be at a chemical disadvantage in our brains that has led to depressive despair; or we have experienced and/or continue to experience a combination of these factors.

Human longing for connection, acceptance and ultimately for love is a gnawing and legitimate hunger. Sometimes we feel we will never have or be 'enough' because our shame and depression have sliced up our soul and cut us off from our neighbours. This piece has tried to show why shame and depression are such a challenge, such mountains to climb; and, by no means definitively, to explore how a spiritual response might provide the support to head towards that hope, that light, that sun.

The most challenging journey we can make is inwards, discovering the contours of our inner life, attempting to scale the sometimes mountainous terrain of our regrets, griefs and loves, hoping that the journey will give us fresh perspective on who we are and how we are to live (Winkett, 2009).

It is my sincere hope that fresh expressions of Church can increasingly be born out of a deep self-knowledge, which first of all takes seriously the addictions we all carry, before seeking to save others. The 12-step path requires the courage necessary for profound existential surrender, but this is a journey the Church, in all its expressions, is called by Christ to follow. Can the Church inspire those who are fearful and in pain – whether within or without its bounds – to let go of all that holds them back and discover that God waits within, trustworthy as a rock, gentle as a child, and surprising as a sunrise? Fresh expressions, with their vocation to build communities specific to the contexts they are called to, must first discover for themselves 'the rock of their salvation' in the midst of their own brokenness. If, as the body of Christ, we can increasingly embark on our own necessary journeys of self-discovery, we will surely become that genuine foretaste of the Kingdom of God, and our mission will flow naturally and effectively to those who have no hope.

References

James Alison, 2006, *Undergoing God*, London: Darton, Longman & Todd

Peter Bates, 1999, *Creating Accepting Communities*, Sarah Dunn (ed.), London: Mind Publications

John Bradshaw, 1988, *Healing the Shame that Binds You*, Florida: Health Communications Inc.

Sally Brampton, 2008, *Shoot the Damn Dog: A Memoir of Depression*, London: Bloomsbury Publishing

Patrick J. Carnes, 1997, *The Betrayal Bond: Breaking Free of Exploitative Relationships*, Florida: Health Communications Inc.

Clare Catford, 2008, 'The Road to Rehab', *Third Way Magazine*, July, 5–6

H. J. Clinebell, 1969, *Basic Types of Pastoral Counselling*, Nashville: Abingdon Press

Larry Culliford, 2007, 'Taking a Spiritual History', in *Advances in Psychiatric Treatment*, Brighton: Brighton Sussex Partnership NHS Trust

Charlotte Davis Kasl, 1990, *Women, Sex and Addiction*, New York: Harper Perennial

John Desmond, 2004, *My One Friend is Darkness: A Lament for Those who Weep*, London: Pen Press Publishers

John Firman and Ann Gila, 1997, *The Primal Wound*, Albany: SUNY Press

Erving Goffman, 1990, *Stigma: Notes on the Management of Spoiled Identity*, London: Penguin Books

Charles Kammer, 1988, *Ethics and Liberation: An Introduction*, London: SCM Press

Paul Lanham, 2005, 'Thoughts from behind a pillar', in Julia Head (ed.), *Bishop John Robinson Fellowship Newsletter*, South London and Maudsley NHS Trust, 16 April, London

Richard Lilly, 2005, 'Service User', in J. Repper and T. Bassett (eds), *Travelling Hopefully*, Mental Health Today, November, pp. 16–18.

Kate Loewenthal, 2007, *Religion, Culture and Mental Health*, Cambridge: Cambridge University Press

Ian Mobsby, 2008, *The Becoming of G-D*, London: YTC Press

Henri J. M. Nouwen, 1975, *Reaching Out*, New York: Doubleday

John O' Donohue, 1998, *Eternal Echoes*, London: Bantam Books

Stephen Pattison, 2000, *Shame: Theory, Therapy, Theology*, Cambridge: Cambridge University Press

Scott M. Peck, 1987, *The Road Less Travelled*, London: Rider

RCP, 2003, *Alcohol and Other Drug Misuse*, online at: http://www.rcpsych.ac.uk/campaigns/changingminds/mentaldisorders/alcoholanddrugmisuse.aspx?theme=print [Accessed 11 June 2012]

RCP, 2003, *Drugs and Alcohol – Whose problem is it anyway? Who cares?* online at: http://www.rcpsych.ac.uk/pdf/whocares.pdf [Accessed 24 February 2012]

Andrew Sims and Christopher C. H. Cooke, 2009, *Spirituality in Psychiatry*, London: Royal College of Psychiatry Publications

John Swinton, 2001, *Spirituality and Mental Health Care*, London: Jessica Kingsley Publishers

Paul Tillich, 2002, *The New Dictionary of Pastoral Studies*, Wesley Carr (ed.), Grand Rapids: Eerdmans

Jean Vanier, 1988, *The Broken Body*, London: Darton, Longman & Todd

Bill W. and Dick B., 1939, *Alcoholics Anonymous: The Big Book*, New York: Alcoholics Anonymous World Services Inc.

Lucy Winkett, 2009, *Thought for the Day* [radio programme], BBC Radio 4, 26 May

Notes

1 Action on Addiction, 2010, *Charities Join Together to Disarm the UK's Biggest Preventable Killer*, online at: www.actiononaddiction.org.uk/News---Publications/News/Charities-Join-Together-to-Disarm-the-UK's-Biggest.aspx [Accessed 24 February 2012].

2 'Steve', no date, *Private discussion forum*, Mental Health World website.

3 Sex and Love Addicts Anonymous, no date, *Signs of Recovery*, online at: http://www.slaaonline.org/readings/#signs Signs of Recovery [Accessed 28 July 2010].

4 Sex and Love Addicts Anonymous, no date, *S.L.A.A. Preamble*, online at: http://www.slaaonline.org/readings/#signs Signs of Recovery [Accessed 28 July 2010].

5 A Sex Addicts Anonymous member sharing privately at a 12-step meeting, August 2009, London.

6 Philip St Romain, 2010, *Twelve Steps to Spiritual Wholeness*, Howard Astin: Lulu Press; and 2002, *12 and a Half Steps to Spiritual Health*, Oxford: Monarch.

15

Poised Between Heaven and Earth

SAM WELLS

Isaiah 65.17–23

I want to tell you about the biggest theological challenge I've faced in ministry. In 1996 I applied to be the vicar of a small church on a housing estate in Norwich, a city of around 130,000 people, one hundred miles north east of London. Norwich was England's second city in the seventeenth century, when the wealth of the wool trade brought it a church for every week of the year and a pub for every day. But the church where I was seeking to become pastor was rather different. Its member-ship numbered around 25 (the regular attendance at worship was smaller) and the neighbourhood it served was the most materially disadvantaged in the east of England. I was excited to be invited to meet the Bishop to discuss the position. It later transpired that I was the only applicant for the job. The Bishop said to me, with disarming frankness, 'Why does a person with a Ph.D. want a job like this?' I replied, 'Because I want to see Jesus and to discover the Kingdom of God. Do you have any suggestions for where Jesus is more likely to show up?'

I grew up in the Church at a time when being radical was easy. Margaret Thatcher was embarking on a series of aus-terity measures that reduced investment in welfare and public services. There were riots in major cities, and the Church of England produced a report called *Faith in the City* that was critical of the government's (and the Church's) neglect of the urban poor.[1] And then Mrs Thatcher defined the era by making her most notorious remark: 'There's no such thing as society.'[2]

You could think yourself radical just by being against Mrs Thatcher.

But by the time I moved to Norwich a decade later there was a new government and a new philosophy. In 1998 Tony Blair announced that seventeen socially disadvantaged areas would be identified and £33 million would be made available to each one if its local residents could organize themselves into a board and committees to run their own regeneration. It turned out my neighbourhood was identified as one of the seventeen.[3] So I found myself taking on a new unpaid additional job as a community organizer and helping to lead a mass democratic regeneration movement for the next 5 years, doing community surveys and elections and training events and big-tent meetings and generally poking our fingers into everything. I chaired the interim group that guided the process until a board was formed. I was then vice-chair of that board until a company limited by guarantee was launched – the first development trust in the Eastern region. I remained as vice-chair until formal elections were held.[4]

And this was the process within which I felt overwhelmed by the biggest theological challenge I've had in ministry. Imagine you're faced with a significant level of social deprivation, and you have pretty much all the money you could dream of to do something about it; you can't blame the government, because they've given you all the help you could ask for. What do you do? Put another way, here is an underclass neighbourhood; it's widely seen around the city and region as a dangerous place that's a drain on more comfortable suburbs and hard-working taxpayers and productive businesses. What would redemption *look* like for such a community? Should you strive to make it look as much like one of the more affluent middle-class suburbs as possible? Is it distinctive only for what it's not, or is there an elixir of life at the heart of the neighbourhood around which can cluster a whole host of initiatives and green shoots of regeneration?

I struggled with that question all through those years – and I've struggled with it ever since. I'd gone to live in the neighbourhood, and I'd got involved in the regeneration process, because I wanted to be with people in their sorrows and struggles, and find beauty and abundance where some might only see shame and scarcity. But then I had to allow my imagination to be stretched to a vision of what it might mean for this community genuinely to flourish, to be happy and settled and at peace with itself. And that was somehow harder.

In some ways what was happening to the community paralleled what was happening to the church of which I was the vicar. When I came to the parish I found a significant divergence of understanding about what the church was called to be. The church building, a multi-purpose meeting space, was only six years old. The members of the congregation were trying to make it look and feel as churchy as they could. But it wasn't working. There was a serviceable organ but no one to play it; a number of local children but no one to run activities for them on Sunday mornings; and an abundance of plump liturgical books but few people with the inclination to read, let alone navigate, them. Thus, like the neighbourhood, the congregation had resources, potential, and tradition, but was less than the sum of its parts and, most of all, lacked self-confidence.

My pastoral experience and my academic training had formed in me the conviction that the key to redemption and to flourishing life lay in the imagination.[5] We act in the world that we see, and we anticipate within the stories that have formed us; but we are often unaware of those stories, because we are surrounded by them as a fish is by the sea. I judged that my role as priest to that congregation was less to fill its soul with more information – education about the Bible and the Church – and more to give it confidence in the Holy Spirit that was already alive and at work in it. Likewise worship should involve rather less of my speaking, and rather more of members of the congregation articulating and exploring and expressing faith and discerning and sharing wisdom. My role was to provide the form more than the content. Liturgy was to become actions, and meditative spaces between them, more than words. When there were words, they were most often sung, so as to make them participatory and memorable.

Inspired by the conscientization process outlined by Paulo

Freire, the broad-based organizing principles of Saul Alinsky, and the Montessori-based pedagogy of Jerome Berryman, I came to see my role as the presenter and re-presenter of the Christian story (scriptural and ecclesial).[6] Most Sundays the centrepiece of worship would be an all-age encounter with a scriptural story. Sometimes it would involve making together a map or chart – for example, we drafted an 'emotional graph' of the narrative of the prodigal and his brother and father. Sometimes it would simply be the presentation of a story found within Berryman's 'Godly Play' scripts, or a customized version of a story in the same spirit. Sometimes it would be a more spontaneous reaction to events. For example, on the Sunday after the US-led invasion of Afghanistan in 2001 I gave everyone a photo-card with a different face on it, and each person placed their photo-card on a large map of Afghanistan and imagined that individual's circumstances in an extended act of lament and intercession. And one Christmas each congregation member took a figure out of the crib scene and explained their reasons for choosing it and its resonance in their own life, before replacing it carefully and prayerfully. Besides providing the frame for these explorations, my own role was to bring them back into genuinely worshipful focus; in particular, I most often concluded the 'time of wondering' by putting the materials or figures tenderly away, one by one, and turning each respective act of 'putting away' into an occasion for petition, praise, penance or thanksgiving that incorporated things spoken in the foregoing interaction.[7]

This style of worship evolved through trial and error and mutual discernment with the congregation and church council. But in my mind I was also trying to foster the little church as a community of imagination, a place where people could explore tentative hopes and articulate memories buried in shallow graves. In particular I sought to make the church a fertile soil for wonder. Wonder is not an indicative statement; nor is it an imperative demand; nor again is it interrogative questioning: a sentence that begins 'I wonder ...' does not have a question mark at the end.[8] It is the land of 'maybe', a land that expands the imagination to apprehend the God that permitted us to be. It is a land in which all that is known is the thread of the gospel story – that the power at the heart of the universe resolved never to be except to be with us, that Jesus is how that power resolved to be with us, that the cross shows us Jesus was prepared to be with us even at the risk of not being with the Trinity, that the resurrection showed us that there is no separating Jesus from God or God from us in Jesus, and that at Pentecost the everything-we-need that God gives us in Jesus, God perpetually continues to give us in the Holy Spirit. That is all that is known – all that 'is'. All else is for wonder and discovery, for reinterpretation and redescription, for reimagining and replaying.

So that little church had everything in place to imagine what social regeneration might mean. But still it wasn't easy. It was a long, extended exercise in discerning what this money could do, what it could catalyse, what it could assist, what it couldn't do, and what it might actually inhibit, complicate or diminish. The Bible, of course, is a storehouse of memory and wisdom on all of these themes.

When the prophets of the Old Testament talked about regeneration and social hope they tended to do it in one of two ways. One way, favoured by the book of Zechariah, was to long for political restoration, to put King David back on the throne and to have Israel king among the nations once again. The other way, portrayed by the book of Daniel, was to imagine a dramatic apocalyptic intervention of God that brought history to an end. You could call the first way earth and the second way heaven. Zechariah's way appealed to an activist spirit; the main drawback was that it was so much about Israel taking its destiny into its own hands that it didn't leave much room for faith in God's action. Daniel's way was all about God's action, but so much so that it encouraged a passive resignation among the people. Little has changed. Those who talk about salvation today tend to be either those who assume it comes from us (so get off your backside) or those who assume it all comes from God (so you might as well stay on your backside).

And that's the context that explains why the vision of Isaiah chapter 65 is so significant and so compelling. It's about God's action. It talks about 'new heavens and a new earth' – so it's obviously about the dramatic and decisive intervention of God. But its details are about children's wellbeing, people building houses and growing crops – things as practical and mundane as a local politician's electoral platform. What's breathtaking about the picture offered in Isaiah 65 is that it's *poised between heaven and earth* – poised between God's action and human action, poised between hope and pragmatism, poised between astonished wonder and hard-won realism, poised between the unknown future and the very ordinary present tense.

Let's look a little more closely at the way Isaiah combines a vision of God and humanity, with each playing its full role in redemption. There are three dimensions to salvation in this description – three answers, if you like, to my question back in Norwich, my question about what it made sense to hope for. The first is about health and wellbeing. 'No more shall there be … an infant that lives but a few days', it says, 'or an old person who does not live out a lifetime.' In the Bible salvation and health are the same thing. Salvation means safety, and permanent relationship with God. If you're anxious about your own health or the health of someone you love, you'll understand exactly how closely salvation and health are connected. You want salvation to make you better. Of course you do.

The second dimension is security – that when you build a house you get to live in it, and when you plant vineyards you get to enjoy their fruit. Two and half thousand years before Karl Marx, Isaiah offers a manifesto for an alternative to slavery or indentured labour or oppressive social structures. Here's a picture of a happy, productive world where everyone gets to make and grow and enjoy and no one has to be exploited or used or alienated. Isaiah assumes it's good to work. This isn't a picture of angels playing harps. Work is at the heart of earth and heaven. There's no better feeling in life than to have good work to do, and to share in doing it with trusted and respected colleagues. Work is at the centre of how human beings turn earth into heaven and bring heaven to earth, blending the gifts of God with the labour of human hands. Just imagine being able to work knowing that your conditions of work would be fertile and all your labours would be fruitful. Isn't that inspiring and energizing? Wouldn't that be a meeting of heaven and earth?

And the third dimension is about the relationship to the soil, to food and to the animals. We get this evocative picture: 'The wolf and the lamb shall feed together, the lion shall eat straw like the ox.' The message here is that the wider relationships that make human habitation possible are not fundamentally conflictual. Isaiah goes on, 'They shall not hurt or destroy on all my holy mountain, says the Lord.' This is the biggest philosophical claim in the whole of Isaiah's vision. It's the promise that when heaven and earth meet there isn't war, but partnership; not battle, but beauty; not a contest for scarce resources, but an act of worship centred around the sharing of food. A Eucharist, perhaps.

So this is Isaiah's answer to my long heart-searching about what to hope for in a disadvantaged neighbourhood. First, foster the right conditions for people's wellbeing – salvation begins with health. Second, make possible constructive, rewarding and fruitful work, so that people may discover the electric excitement of enjoying the work of their own hands. And third, heal relationships, between people and each other, people and animals, and people and the soil.

In some ways, this was exactly what I tried to do in that parish. When I came to the parish, there was a lot of vandalism taking place on the church building – which stretched back to the extended period of the building's construction, when the site became an adventure playground for fearless local children. Stones were periodically thrown at the building during worship, services were sometimes interrupted by mischievous and assertive young people, and very occasionally congregation members were subject to stone throwing or theft. So getting a healthy and safe relationship between the church and the local young people was the top priority. The second move was to find and affirm useful roles for congregation members to fulfil in the community, fragile as the lives of many of them were. And the third was to embark on a more ambitious programme of telling truthful stories and making reconciliation within the neighbourhood and between the neighbourhood and other parts of the city.

This is a pretty comprehensive manifesto. It's not other-worldly and out of touch, but it's not so down to earth that it's easily within reach. It's poised between heaven and earth. But it's missing one thing that's laced throughout Isaiah's vision. When I was helping to organize the housing estate in Nor-wich, I would often be bewildered that there was no place for faith in our conversations. We would have big meetings with huge challenges, but we would never start with a prayer. That meant we were simply relying on our own strength. We had squabbles about whose work was recognized in the media and celebrated in the community. But we had no way of talking about whose work most closely resembled God's Kingdom. I found that work exhausting in a way I've never found church work exhausting, because we had no hands but our own to work with. But Isaiah infuses his vision with the presence of God. God is more intimately involved in redemption than the people themselves. God says, 'Before they call I will answer, while they are yet speaking I will hear.' Have you ever been understood like that? Isn't that the most thrilling description of God, as one who knows our thoughts and our interests and our flourishing better than we do, but lets us enjoy the work of our hands anyway? Most wonderfully of all, God says, 'I am about to create Jerusalem as a *joy*, and its people as a *delight*. I will *rejoice* in Jerusalem, and *delight* in my people.' Is there any feeling in heaven or earth more fabulous than to know that your life is God's delight? Isn't that the epitome of heaven – the discovery that God shapes his whole life for your flourishing – that God's joy is *you*?

I look back ten years and think, if I'd spent a little more time with Isaiah, I might have felt a clearer answer to my question. Bodily wellbeing, creative and fruitful labour, healthy interper-sonal, political and environmental relationships: this really is a manifesto for any kind of people, however varied the realities or their economic or social circumstances. But now I see what I was struggling with wasn't fundamentally or specifically about poverty. It was about what we are each to hope for in this life, and what it means to strive for flourishing life in God's Kingdom. I was trying to discover what it means to long for God's transformation, and yet take active small steps in the meantime to imitate the wellbeing, fruitfulness and harmony that only God can finally bring. In other words, what it means to be poised between heaven and earth.

How's Isaiah's vision working out for you right now? Are you healthy, and is your body at peace with itself? Is your work fruitful and are you able to enjoy the fruit of your hands? Are you at peace with your environment and are the wolf and the lamb in your life feeding together? And is your life one that makes God say, 'You are my joy and delight'?

These are the things we long for one another. When we wave a child off to college or get a Christmas letter from a friend or call a grandparent to get the latest news, these are the things we most deeply yearn to know. This was the closest I got to an answer to my question. Working out the specifics was a project we never completed together. But the experience of being near enough to see Isaiah's agenda but always knowing it to be out of reach is precisely to be poised between heaven and earth, to live in God's grace but always to hope in God's promise.

I have two friends who've known each other for thirty years and meet up for a weekend about once a year. As soon as they see each other after many months apart, they always ask each other the same question: 'Are you living well?' It's a question about a sound body, fruitful work, healthy relationships, and a life lived in God's joy. Maybe that's the question I should have been asking back in Norwich on that housing project. Maybe that's the question Isaiah has for those of us seeking to build contextual expressions of Christian community, whether our context is one of material wealth or poverty, hopefulness or fearfulness, flourishing or struggling. Perhaps the question Isaiah would ask regarding our missional endeavours is, 'What does "living well" look like for this context, these people? How can this community be poised between heaven and earth?'

Notes

1 Archbishop of Canterbury's Commission on Urban Priority Areas, 1985, *Faith in the City: A Call for Action by Church and Nation*, 1985, London: Church House Publishing.

2 'I think we have gone through a period when too many children and people have been given to understand "I have a problem, it is the Government's job to cope with it!" or "I have a problem, I will go and get a grant to cope with it!"; "I am homeless, the Government must house me!" and so they are casting their problems on society and who is society? *There is no such thing!* There are individual men and women and there are families and no government can do anything except through people and people look to themselves first.' 'If children have a problem, it is society that is at fault. *There is no such thing as society.* There is a living tapestry of men and women and people and the beauty of that tapestry and the quality of our lives will depend upon how much each of us is prepared to take responsibility for ourselves and each of us prepared to turn round and help by our own efforts those who are unfortunate.' 'Aids, education and the year 2000!' Interview conducted by Douglas Keay, *Woman's Own*, 31 October, 1987, pp. 8–10.

3 For a wider background and evaluation, see http://www.communities.gov.uk/publications/communities/afinalassessment

4 I offer a detailed account of this experience in my *Community-Led Estate Regeneration and the Local Church*, 2003, Cambridge: Grove Booklets. See also Samuel Wells, 'Generation, Degeneration, Regeneration: The Theological Architecture and Horticulture of a Deprived Housing Estate', *Political Theology* 3/2, 2002, pp. 238–44; and 'No Abiding Inner City: A New Deal for the Church', in Mark Thiessen Nation and Samuel Wells (eds), *Faithfulness and Fortitude: In Conversation with Stanley Hauerwas*, 2000, Edinburgh: T & T Clark.

5 See especially Samuel Wells, *Improvisation: The Drama of Christian Ethics*, 2004, Grand Rapids: Brazos; London: SPCK.

6 See Paulo Freire, *Pedagogy of the Oppressed*, 2003, New York: Continuum; Saul D. Alinsky, *Rules for Radicals: A Pragmatic Primer for Realistic Radicals*, 1989, New York: Vintage; and Jerome W. Berryman, *The Complete Guide to Godly Play*, 7 volumes, 2008, Denver: Morehouse.

7 For a longer account of this ministry, see Samuel Wells, 'Imagination', in Samuel Wells and Sarah Coakley (eds), *Praying for England: Priestly Presence in Contemporary Culture*, 2008, London and New York: Continuum, pp. 65–84.

8 David Ford explores such modes of speech and their theological valence in his *The Future of Christian Theology*, 2001, Oxford: Wiley-Blackwell, pp. 68–83.

16

Afterword

THE EDITORS

The contributors to this collection offer a variety of perspectives around a shared conviction that it is not possible to talk about the Church of God without reference to the Kingdom of God, and vice versa. This conviction is supported from different theological perspectives, and by practitioners from a range of contexts in the UK and the USA. But at the heart is a shared commitment that new and old communities of Christian faith are to be communities of the kingdom and therefore of social transformation.

But this is not a general book about the Church and social change. It is a book about the current practice and future potential of some fledgling Christian communities – fresh expressions of Church – to share in that ministry, and to make a distinctive contribution to it.

The purpose of the Church

In an article that anticipated many of today's challenges and controversies about mission, Lesslie Newbigin wrote that the purpose of the Church, in its local form, was to be 'for the place where it is located ... in the light of God's purposes in Christ for that place' (1971, p. 4).

Understood in this way no local church should live for itself, but for Christ in its local community. But that community does not directly set the local church's agenda, although its needs are to be taken with great seriousness. It is the transformation that Christ offers that place that shapes the Church's priorities.

This involves a double act of translation. 'Seeking to translate the good news afresh, it seeks at the same time to "translate" the world around, to *re-locate* it in the context of God's new creation' (Williams, p. 11). This translation and transformation, both synonyms for the impact of the Kingdom of God, is to be understood holistically. It is an 'integral mission'[1] involving all the marks of mission (Introduction, p. xv). Drawing from Isaiah's vision of a new heaven and new earth, Sam Wells identified this as wellbeing, security, fruitful work and healed relationships, demonstrated in a community 'caught between heaven and earth'.[2] Angell reminds us that 'the kingdom is inseparably connected to justice.'[3] Freeman writes of 'an axis of prayer, mission and justice'. For Cray, Wright and others, signs of the kingdom must be signs of hope. 'The kingdom is the life in which we are called out of our routines' to see 'Paradise in Peckham' (Wright, p. 144). For Archbishop Rowan, *'The Church exists to manifest the new humanity, the restored image'* (p. 3).

An integral approach to mission is not only integrated, in the sense that no dimension is excluded or downplayed; it also requires that each dimension be allowed its own integrity. Faith sharing must not be manipulative nor issues of human need be engaged manipulatively (Angell, p. 123). In terms of the 'fresh expressions journey' (Cray, p. 19), 'loving and serving' is not for the sake of 'exploring discipleship'. It is what Christians do, and thus demonstrates true discipleship.

Understood in this way, the Church's vocation as a sign, instrument and foretaste of that kingdom (Cray, pp. 17f.) is to be both local and contextual. But each of these terms is problematic.

Local mission

The local, however, is not what it used to be! Newbigin recognizes that 'place' is complicated; that most westerners live in a plurality of places (1971, p. 5), as work has been separated from home, and mobility becomes the norm for the majority, and its absence a mark of poverty and exclusion for the trapped minority. Mobility allows community based on networks of common interest to create bonds that are sometimes stronger than those of neighbourhoods. Finally, a pluralistic society, made up of competing world views, and an individualizing society of consumer choice, can fragment local community. Yet a kingdom-shaped concern is for all and for the whole. In the UK, Anglican clergy share with their bishop 'the cure of souls', meaning a responsibility before God for the spiritual wellbeing of everyone who lives in the parish; other Christian traditions have similar concerns. We are not just there for people who come to church, and the changing nature of the local means that many traditional models of Church are limited in their reach. One size fits all is no longer adequate for contemporary Western communities. It is here that fresh expressions of Church play a vital part. They complement historic ministry and reach networks, neighbourhoods and constituencies of concern, which would otherwise remain substantially untouched by the local churches' existing work. They have a 'go to' missiology, rather than a 'come to us' expectation.

In this volume these include multi-racial Peckham (Wright), multi-faith Birmingham (Sudworth), those trapped in addiction in County Antrim (Paynter) or London (Catford), a university campus in San Diego (Angell), deprived estates in Llanfair Penrhys (Williams), Vancouver (Freeman) and Winchester (Kennedy), people who have to work on public holidays in Denver (Bolz-Weber), street sleepers in Reading (Freeman), new housing developments in Glasgow and London, a block of flats in Portsmouth, the night-time economy in Wolverhampton, a farmers' market in Walthamstow, vulnerable youth in Chard, a residents' association in Dartford, environmental concern, and those whose lives are impaired by disabilities, in Deal, the rural poor in Newcastleton and the urban poor in Sheffield, 'Ragamuffins' and bikers in Swansea, young families in Howden Clough, and so on (Cray). All aim to be 'a refuge to people trapped by all kinds of trouble' (Paynter) in their various contexts.

The mixed economy

Most of these are new Christian communities; a few are churches that have turned themselves inside out (Wells and Sudworth). They represent 'a more expansive ecclesiology – an ecclesiology that points to what it means to be Church outside of just worship services and committees' (Bolz-Weber, p. 52). All complement, in one way or another, the ministry of other churches or congregations in a mixed economy, which Lincoln Harvey tells us is 'an appropriate reflection on the liveliness of God' (p. 102). Harvey also warns us against allowing a spirit of competition to distort our approach to the mixed economy partnership, of the danger of an 'overheated' internal debate that detracts from a kingdom focus (p. 97). In the history of the Church and of Christian mission 'neither continuity nor change "wins"' (p. 103). Where the 'heat' of the debate comes from dissatisfaction or painful encounters with inherited Church, this must be acknowledged; through the God or redemption it can be turned into 'creative dissatisfaction' (Williams, p. 2) for the sake of mission.

This mixed economy partnership guards against the danger that fresh expressions might just increase the fragmentation of the Church, rather than extend its reach through a principled diversity within unity. In the light of Phyllis Tickle's accurate diagnosis that 'Like ... previous eras of massive change, we too are facing ancient quandaries from within a new context' (p. 61), a remarkable feature of the fresh expressions movement, in the UK at least, is the partnership of inherited Church and fresh expressions of Church. Each needs the other. Richard Sudworth describes 'a huge sense of permission' and sees fresh expressions as 'the inherited Church's reconfigured presence' (p. 29).

Contextual mission

If 'local' provides a missional challenge, so too does 'contextual'. Fresh expressions involve 'building new ecclesial communities out of contextual mission' (Introduction, p. xiv), but context is more than the local. The Church's stance against injustice will properly also be at a national level, but national and international injustice always take local form somewhere. Every context is 'glocal' (Cray, p. 27). As Damian Feeney says, 'There are invariably local manifestations of global issues that affect small groups of people and for which a voice is needed. Additionally, 'global issues are global precisely because they affect everyone' (Feeney, p. 128). So context is where the global or national impacts the local. Contextual mission involves 'the constant challenge to follow Christ without any separation between public and private' (Sudworth, p. 36). It should be characterized by 'local advocacy for the worth of each person and of the common good' (Feeney, p. 136).

The capacity and potential of fresh expressions to be signs, agents and foretastes of the kingdom does not mean that they all automatically fulfil that potential. Why should we assume that fledgling Christian communities will escape the pitfalls of self-preservation and homogeneity that also afflict more established forms of church life? 'The question of eclecticism remains as an issue throughout the whole Church' (Feeney, p. 131).

Best practice is being learned the hard way, at the interface of Church, kingdom and context. 'Fresh expressions of Church do not drop down, fully formed, from the sky. In common with the life of the whole Church, they are in the process of becoming, and it will be through the stories and emerging praxis of fresh expressions that criticisms are either answered or ignored' (Feeney, p. 135).

Contextual mission is both demanding and costly. 'The new mission agenda seeks to take seriously the *strangeness* of the world at large. It accepts that in order to speak the Word of God effectively in an unfamiliar context, you will have to let the Word of God itself become 'strange' to you and discover it all over again in someone else's language and culture (Williams, p. 2). At its heart is a commitment to an incarnational approach – a willingness to stay in 'someone else's language and culture' so as to rediscover the gospel in and for it. This cannot be achieved by an attractional approach, which requires 'the other' to come to me and discover the faith in my language, not theirs.

Discernment

Within this incarnational praxis imaginative and prayerful discernment is foundational. Sam Wells described Church as 'a community of imagination' (p. 165). Paul Kennedy describes prayer-walking 'to become immersed in God's activity in this place' and to provide the raw material for 'developing contextual theology' (pp. 44f.). Discerning prayer will undergird the whole lifespan of any fresh expression that understands itself as a sign of the kingdom. It will aim to develop a praxis of community, prayer, service and theologizing. Andy Freeman draws on the international experience of the 24-7 Prayer movement when he says, 'It seems that when people commit to pray, God opens their eyes to the needs of the environment they live in and sends them out to make a difference' (p. 108).

The first answers discerned in this process may prove to be half-truths or projections. Kennedy warns of the need of perseverance and the likelihood of 'false starts' before finding the right process (p. 41). Patience is needed during the process of initial discernment. More patience than most practitioners expect! 'It is a slow and patient exercise in discovering what can and can't be heard' (Williams, p. 6).

Discipleship

Sam Wells' question, 'What does "living well" look like for this context?' is an excellent key to such prayer (p. 170). But it also introduces further questions: what should discipleship look like in this context? And how are such disciples formed? Or Feeney's questions of how 'new Christian communities are formed, in such a way that the values of the kingdom are rendered explicit' (p. 127), and whether 'fresh expressions [can] be places where personal identities and attitudes are challenged and transformed, rather than merely affirmed and accepted' (p. 130). And even more profoundly perhaps, Rowan Williams asks, 'How can fresh expressions 'challenge the corporate imagination of their social context?' (p. 5).

Catford and Paynter both recognize the profoundly addictive nature of contemporary Western society, and that this requires the Church to 'rethink the meaning of disciple[ship]' if churches are to bring freedom to the addicted (Paynter, p. 83). Catford points to a variety of 12-step processes that originated from the Church and that churches can re-appropriate (p. 155). A growing number of fresh expressions and missional communities are developing a rule of life, or a community ethos. As Archbishop Rowan describes, 'The basic characteristics of the life of Llanfair Penrhys, the church centre on the estate, had to do with communal ministry, service and depth of spiritual discipline, plus growth in prayer, contribution to wider society, and to teach and learn from one another' (p. 7). In its cultural context, the whole environment of a fresh expression of Church needs to be that of a community of whole-life disciples, rather than an event to attend (Cray, p. 25). Pope Benedict's encyclical identifies the object of these transformational processes as 'The forming of conscience, the stimulation of insight, the readiness to act' (Feeney, p. 132).

Public worship

At the heart of this transforming environment is worship. Worship might be described as the sixth mark of mission. Fresh expressions best develop into public worshipping communities, rather than start with a public act of worship (Cray, p. 25). But the intention is contextually appropriate public worship. 'The creative shift that is required is in the fusing of worship, Christian spirituality and practical service in a way that is recognizable to the surrounding community' (Sudworth, p. 35).

There is no Church in the absence of Word and sacraments. The Church itself is a sacrament, a foretaste of the Kingdom of God. And the Eucharist, the central act of Christian worship, is the feast of the kingdom community, the anticipation of the final banquet in the new heavens and earth. So Feeney asks, 'Can fresh expressions find an appropriate and creative balance between creative innovation and the ecclesial rootedness of the Eucharist?' (p. 134).

Certainly for Toby Wright, Glorious – 'the fragile beginning of an urban fresh expression that recognized sacraments as evangelistic tools and enabled the young people within our communities to engage with the church from wherever they happen to be' (p. 145) – was a demonstration of the kingdom, through a eucharistic community. 'When we have our sacramental teaching and practice clear, we are likely to have our transformational social vision clear as well' (Williams, p. 9).

Potential

Fresh expressions of Church are already being agents of transformation for the Kingdom of God. With continuing support – the 'huge sense of permission', with careful reflection on missionary practice, with contextual patterns of formation for discipleship and with mature public worship, they have the chance to be and do far more.

References

Lesslie Newbigin, 1971, 'What is "a Local Church truly United"?', *The Ecumenical Review*, online at: http://www.wcc-coe.org/wcc/who/crete-03-e.html [Accessed 30 March 2012]

Notes

1 See Tim Chester (ed.), *Justice, Mercy and Humility: Integral Mission and the Poor*, 2002, Milton Keynes: Paternoster.

2 A similar vision is found in Raymond Fung, *The Isaiah Vision: An Ecumenical Strategy for Congregational Evangelism*, Faith and Order Papers, Worldwide Council of Churches.

3 See Chris Howson, *A Just Church: 21st Century Liberation Theology in Action*, 2011, London: Continuum.